On my wedding day I received horrible news. My dad was leaving my mom for another woman. Dad told my new husband just as we were pulling out for our honeymoon because he didn't want me to be surprised when I returned  ached when I read Sue Birdseye's story winter to the soul, but Sue turned to G odness, and watered her pain with His w ... God is meeting her still. Sue's message of help and hope is a must-read for those wintering the loss of a marriage.

—Tricia Goyer
Author of thirty-four books, including the co-authored
book *Lead Your Family Like Jesus*

Anyone struggling with the pain of spousal abandonment needs a friend to walk the journey with them. Sue wants to be that friend to you or someone you know experiencing the rejection of divorce. She knows how you feel. Her words will help you know you are not alone. I'm amazed at her remarkable faith, her tenacity to keep going each day, and her sense of humor to keep laughing in spite of her circumstances. Read her story and share it liberally with the many others who need it.

—Barbara Rainey
Co-founder of FamilyLife, author, artist, creator of
www.EverThineHome.com, mother of six, grandmother of 19

With personal experience and Biblical insight, Sue Birdseye shares how to navigate the complex journey of divorce and single parenting. *When Happily Ever After Shatters* provides Christian wisdom and day-to-day comfort for the person experiencing the death of his or her marriage.

—Laura Petherbridge
International speaker and author of *When I Do Becomes
I Don't—Practical Steps for Healing During Separation
or Divorce* and *The Smart Stepmom*

This is the *best* book I've read this year. Disarmingly honest, full of hope, and immensely practical. A great read for everyone, not just those whose marriages have failed. No trite answers, just real honesty. A courageous book. Get five copies. One for yourself and four to give away!

—SUSAN YATES

International speaker and author of thirteen books,
including *Raising Kids with Character That Lasts*

When Happily Ever After Shatters

Seeing God in the Midst of Divorce & Single Parenting

Sue Birdseye

Foreword by bestselling author SHAUNTI FELDHAHN

TYNDALE HOUSE PUBLISHERS, INC., CAROL STREAM, ILLINOIS

A Focus on the Family book published by
Tyndale House Publishers, Inc., Carol Stream, Illinois 60188

Focus on the Family and the accompanying logo and design are federally registered trademarks.
Focus on the Family, Colorado Springs, CO 80995.

TYNDALE and Tyndale's quill logo are registered trademarks of Tyndale House Publishers, Inc.

Editor: Brandy Bruce
Cover design by Erik M. Peterson
Cover photograph of plant copyright © Florea Marius Catalin/iStockphoto. All rights reserved.

Library of Congress Cataloging-in-Publication Data
Birdseye, Sue.
  When happily ever after shatters : seeing God in the midst of divorce and single parenting / Sue Birdseye.— First edition.
      pages cm
  Includes bibliographical references (pages   ) and index.
  ISBN 978-1-58997-734-1 (alk. paper)
  1. Divorced people—Religious life. 2. Single parents—Religious life. I. Title.
  BV4596.D58B57 2013
  248.8'46—dc23
                                        2012040804

Printed in the United States of America
1 2 3 4 5 6 7 8 9 / 18 17 16 15 14 13

This book is dedicated with more love than words
could convey to my sweet children,
Zachary, Emma, Peter, Elizabeth, and Allison.
I pray that each of you "being rooted
and established in love, may have power,
together with all the saints, to grasp how wide
and long and high and deep is the love of Christ,
and to know this love that surpasses knowledge—
that you may be filled to the measure of all the fullness of God."
(Ephesians 3:17–19, ESV)

Contents

FOREWORD

There is a great—and currently unmet—need in the Christian community for a book that offers life, hope, healing, and practical guidance for those who are facing the shock of abandonment in their marriage. A book written not by a counselor or a psychologist but by a wise Christian woman who has gone through it, who couldn't find such a book when she needed it most, and who has been walking the journey toward her own healing with an eye for how God can use her story to help others.

The problem of abandonment is far more widespread than many realize, and up until now it has been in the shadows. What does a spouse do when the usual Christian resources about how to fight for your marriage no longer apply? How does one face a spouse's unfaithfulness and desertion with a Christlike perspective, both for one's own sake and, often, for the sake of one's children? These are questions Christian counselors hear from women and men every day, yet there are few written resources to serve as a healthy biblical companion on such a road.

I believe Sue Birdseye is the perfect woman to write this book. Sue was my closest friend growing up. We were in each other's weddings and spent many hours together as couples, delighting in each other's children—in her case, five children, two of which she and her then-husband adopted from foster care. There was no way that her husband, this godly, wonderful man I knew, a public figure, would have ever cheated on his beautiful, delightful, homeschooling wife . . . and yet, he did. He left her and their children for another woman. Sue fought for the marriage, but in the end, she had no choice in the matter. He was done.

Since then, I have known others who have faced abandonment and unwanted divorces. I meet these people every week at my events. They call in when I'm on radio programs. Having never gone through this heartbreak myself, I can't truly help them. But Sue has and she can.

I am proud of my friend for walking this shocking road with grace, courage, and a determination to avoid bitterness, even when it would be understandable. I am touched by her ability to find life, encouragement, and even humor in a very humorless situation. And based on my eight years of research on men, women, and marriages, I know that a book with that tone will comfort and help the many thousands of others who find themselves on the same journey.

—SHAUNTI FELDHAHN

Social researcher, speaker, and bestselling author of *For Women Only: What You Need to Know about the Inner Lives of Men*

ONE

Ambushed by Adultery

God is our refuge and strength, an ever-present help in trouble.
Therefore we will not fear, though the earth give way and the
mountains fall into the heart of the sea, though its waters roar
and foam and the mountains quake with their surging.

—PSALM 46:1–3

It was my own personal 9/11. A beautiful day, not a cloud in the sky, birds chirping, children playing—when out of nowhere disaster struck with six words uttered by my husband: "I think I'm going to leave."

With those six words came the end of my world as I knew it. But let me backtrack for a moment. Before I tell you my story of abandonment and divorce, let me share with you my love story.

My husband and I met at a Bible study on the book of Revelation. (I'm sure there's a really good end-time joke there somewhere!) He was an engaging, handsome, intelligent man, and he definitely caught my eye.

I didn't realize he had any interest in me until a few weeks later at one of the Bible-study meetings when he sat down next to me on the sofa and struck up a conversation. We soon were choosing each other's company at more and more church events. We found we had a lot in common and enjoyed talking about our faith, politics, and our shared interests.

After the Bible study ended, we continued to do things together as friends. I say that, but looking back I might have been a bit naive to think that was the extent of our interest in each other. He had just turned thirty and was seven years older than I. One night after we had spent a few months getting to know each other, he asked me what I thought a thirty-year-old man would be looking for in a relationship.

I said something like, "Someone to hang out with?"

He said, "No, I'm looking for the woman I will marry."

I was surprised but replied, "Well, whatever God wants is fine. I'm happy being friends and would be open to this turning into something more."

He shared later that my response actually made him like me more. He said he was attracted to my confidence. The nature of our relationship didn't change immediately. I hadn't planned on dating anyone at the time, so it took a little bit longer for me to wrap my brain around him as husband material.

One particular night he graciously ate two slices of the worst apple pie I had ever made. While watching him eat that horrible pie with a smile on his face, I knew I was falling in love. Then he leaned over and kissed me. The man had just eaten the worst thing I'd ever made, and two helpings at that! I had to kiss him back!

A few months later, on the Saturday before Easter, he professed his love for me. I shared that I loved him as well. Within the year we were engaged and married. I used to be proud to share our love story, but now after what has happened, I'm slightly embarrassed to share how quickly we were married. And yet I was truly blessed to be happily married . . . until the day I wasn't.

The next seventeen years were filled with children, foster care, adoption, city management, church, homeschooling, community involvement, and life. Our home was happy, but as anyone with a family of five children will tell you (if he or she is being honest), it was chaotic joy. I won't say I had it all together because I didn't, but I did try. I passionately, but not perfectly, loved and respected my husband. I loved being married and taking care of my family, with all the struggles and joys that entailed.

There was no great season of tumult. There were no warning skirmishes, battles, or war cries. Only an ambush. There was no discussion of difficulties, disappointments, or impending disasters. There was just my simple question, "Hey, why did it take you so long to pick up your dry cleaning?" And my husband's answer, "I think I'm going to leave."

As my five children and their friends raced around us playing, blissfully unaware of the tragedy that was unfolding, I stood staring at the man I loved with tears streaming down my cheeks. Inside I was crying out in fear and disbelief, but what actually came out of my mouth were only shocked, whispered questions. He was unaffected and stoic. He gave me nothing concrete, no reason, and even denied the existence of another woman. I chose to believe him.

I was terribly misled. It took me days to determine there was more to the situation than I originally believed. As I fought desperately for my family, my husband withdrew more and more—and acted guiltier and guiltier. It didn't take long for me to demand he come clean. At first he described the other woman as an acquaintance he found intriguing and was thinking about pursuing. Still, I felt there was more to the story.

A few mornings later, as we prepared for our day, I asked again about the woman. He literally ran out of our house, jumped in his car, and sped away. I called his office to no avail. When I did get in touch with his secretary, she said he was locked in his office and wasn't receiving calls. I insisted she let him know I was on the phone. Thankfully, he took my call. Over the phone he shared that he had met someone else, but she was just a good friend. He implied it was an innocent friendship. I asked that he end it. He said he would think about it.

This might seem hard to believe, but I felt relatively calm at this point. I thought that I might indeed be getting the truth. Oddly, it was a relief. Unfortunately, I was again being duped, but I didn't discover the truth until later.

That evening I dressed up and went to one of my husband's weekly city council meetings. I made sure to look as attractive as I could. I sat down right in his line of vision. He looked extremely uncomfortable and wouldn't even glance my way. When the meeting ended, his staff all greeted me with smiles and kind words. Many said, "We're so surprised you stayed for such a long meeting!" Long meeting? Were they kidding? It was only ten o'clock! I had always thought the meetings went much later, sometimes until one or two o'clock in the morning. Oh my. I really had been fooled.

A few days later, on the sidelines at my oldest daughter's field hockey practice, he spilled the whole sordid tale. It was horrible and more shockingly painful than I can describe. What I had hoped was simply a fling was so much more. While we watched my daughter play, he shared about his relationship with this other woman. They had been together physically, and he thought he loved her. I was devastated.

I don't remember what I said in response. I just remember quickly grabbing our eighteen-month-old daughter, rushing to the car, calling a friend, and weeping like I never had before. The rest of the day and the next day and the next were a blur. My children stayed with friends, my husband continued life as if everything was normal, and I tried to figure out what to do. I tried to make a battle plan.

I called our pastors, who tried to talk sense into my husband. The few friends who did know the situation tried to convince him to stop the insanity, but he was indifferent. It seemed as though he had turned off his emotions. Everyone who spent time with him had the same story. They shared that he listened without response and seemed unaffected by anything they said. He was a completely different man from the one they had known for so long.

Close friends of ours urgently reminded him of the importance and value of our family, but he no longer treasured us. No amount of talking could influence him. This other woman had captured his attention and, it appeared, his heart as well. He told some of our friends that he felt bonded to her and considered her his soul mate. I had become nothing to him.

For the next several weeks, I begged, pleaded, changed what I thought might help, prayed, and wept. I didn't kick him out for fear he would never come back. I knew whose house he would go to, and that, frankly, wasn't an option. Although he said he was considering what to do, I think I knew that in his heart he had already left.

Despite the fact that he seemed to love someone else and had obviously shut down his emotions regarding me and our children, over time I came to believe that he didn't want to be the one who officially ended our marriage. I learned from our counselor and my attorney that adulterers often don't make the final move to end the marriage. Sadly, it's the betrayed spouse who is forced to make that difficult decision. I found that to be the case for us. (I'll share more about that process later.)

Strangely, based on some of the things my husband said, I wondered if he also thought he might be able to keep us all. I learned that this, too, wasn't a completely uncommon behavior for adulterers. In their view, they had been able to have it all up to the point of being caught, so why wouldn't everyone be willing to continue with the arrangement? My husband's behavior was clouding his ability to think rationally and realistically. Thankfully, my vision was clear, and my next step was to arrange for marriage counseling and for the two of us to attend a marriage conference.

He was willing to go to both, but he didn't participate in either. He was basically just a body on the counseling sofa—warm body, cold heart. Despite this setback, I was undeterred in my efforts to get through to him. Every day I tried to talk to him about the hope I had for restoration. I tried to convince him that God had planned for us to be together. I reminded him of our vows, of our life together, of our children. It was our life to be lived together. He was not God's best for this other woman.

It was like reasoning with a rock. I kept thinking he would respond. I couldn't reconcile that this man, who had been my best friend, partner, and lover, suddenly was my betrayer. I kept remembering our life together. Only days before everything exploded, we'd been laughing so hard that we ended up practically sitting on the kitchen floor with tears streaming down our faces. How had we gotten to this point? I was baffled.

The pain of betrayal was more physical than I could have ever imagined. I couldn't eat or sleep. The thought of swallowing anything past the giant lump in my throat was daunting. I was definitely on the adultery diet—effective but not recommended. Every time I lay down at night, I would end up fighting thoughts of fear and despair. I would lie there beside my husband and feel hopelessness wash over me. It was completely surreal in so many ways, and all too real in others.

This man who had slept beside me for more than seventeen years was now unrecognizable. This man who had been a leader and teacher in our church was no longer walking with the Lord. This man who was the father of our five children was daily pulling further and further away from them. And I was discovering that no matter how desperately I wanted to change him and our circumstances, I was unable to do much at all.

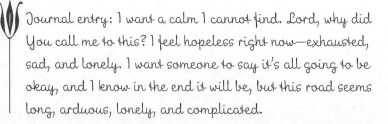

Journal entry: I want a calm I cannot find. Lord, why did You call me to this? I feel hopeless right now—exhausted, sad, and lonely. I want someone to say it's all going to be okay, and I know in the end it will be, but this road seems long, arduous, lonely, and complicated.

Regardless, I resolved to not give up on my marriage. It was no easy resolution. Betrayal was like no pain I could have imagined and responding in kindness was incredibly difficult. I did all I could to offer grace to him, to treat him respectfully, and to love him despite his behavior. I definitely didn't do it flawlessly. I struggled, but I felt that this was what I was supposed to do—until God showed me otherwise. I hoped God was going to do something mighty and miraculous, which to me meant restoring my marriage and my family.

I believed that God would bless my efforts because I was striving to be a godly wife to an adulterer. That warranted something pretty amazing from God, didn't it? That might not have been the best motivation, although I did honestly feel that God was leading me to love my husband regardless of his actions. I was hopeful that I could love him back to me.

To be perfectly honest, at times it still feels as if all my attempts to save my marriage were for naught, but I know they weren't. Like many people in this situation, I didn't receive the outcome I desired, but I did begin to understand myself and my relationship with the Lord on a much deeper level. And while it was a day-by-day, step-by-step, remind-myself-to-breathe kind of experience, I saw that God was (and continues to be) with me, helping me maintain a Christ-centered perspective even during the worst times.

MARCHING FORWARD

I believe that God's perfect will is that all marriages stay intact (Matthew 19:5–6), that we love each other always, that we keep our marriage beds pure (Hebrews 13:4), and that we raise our children to love and follow the Lord (Ephesians 6:4). I also believe we live in a fallen world, where our choices have consequences. There is no doubt that the actions of my ex-husband had negative consequences on my children and me, but there is life after adultery and divorce. I am proof.

My story is unbelievable, at least to me. There are still days when I shake my head in disbelief, but I no longer struggle so much with the troublesome thoughts that plagued me early on, such as, *I can't believe my husband was an adulterer! Am I really divorced? How did this happen? What happened to the man I married? Was it me? What did I do wrong? How am I going to walk my children through this? Will I survive this life? Oh, God, help!*

Maybe you're dealing with all those thoughts and asking yourself and God those same questions. Maybe you're where I was a few years ago—stunned, in the initial stages of grief, wondering, *Oh, God, how am I going to do this?* Maybe you are, like I am now, a single parent looking for answers for how to do this task you weren't really made to do—to be both Mom and Dad. Perhaps you're a friend of someone in this situation, hoping to find trustworthy biblical information on how to help him or her through this ordeal.

Unfortunately for me, none of my friends had the real-world experience with abandonment to help me understand all the eventualities. They loved me well, supported me completely, and blessed me immeasurably, but none of us were equipped to deal with the onslaught of issues adultery and divorce presented. Over the years I had met quite a few women who had been through divorces, but I hadn't considered asking specific questions about their situations and how they got through them successfully. I certainly hadn't gleaned any information that would have prepared me for a situation I never thought I'd be in.

Though friends at my church stepped up and tried to help prevent our divorce, they weren't sure how to guide me through the process once it was clear that it was going to happen. Even a biblically supported divorce is difficult to navigate. Others wanted to advise me from a worldly perspective that just struck me as wrong. Even Christians can be vindictive and mean when provoked, and I didn't want to be that kind of Christian. Also, I had five children looking to me for help, comfort, and stability. It was more than important that I determine not only how to survive this tumultuous situation but how to succeed in marching forward as well.

A BATTLE PLAN TO SHARE

My purpose in writing this book is to share my journey and offer you hope and a path to healing. I won't be able to provide a definitive five-point plan for surviving unwanted abandonment and divorce—because there isn't one. But whether you are the abandoned spouse or that person's friend, mentor, or counselor, I can take your hand and walk with you through this agonizing and arduous ordeal. Everyone's situation is different, but all spouses going through the experience of abandonment and divorce feel the same pain and need the same healing. And if you're going through this, or have gone through it, I want to encourage you that there is hope for those of us who have known the sting of betrayal and the ache of abandonment.

As I share my story, I pray you'll see that even in the midst of great pain, there is potential for great miracles. I've found that when life is beyond difficult, strength and peace are available through Christ. On both a practical and emotional level, each stage of the healing process is its own battle. In the pages ahead, we will tread carefully through the aftermath of abandonment and the minefield of divorce to the victory that lies ahead. I cannot promise you ease, comfort, or pain-free living. But I can promise this:

1. God is "able to do immeasurably more than all we ask or imagine" (Ephesians 3:20). After my husband left and was subsequently fired

because of his adultery, I feared that I wouldn't be able to take care of my children. In desperation I prayed that God would enable me to provide for us, and within a few months, I secured a job at a Christian school, where my four youngest children were welcomed as students. My two-year-old was cared for across the hall from my classroom, and my three-year-old was two doors down the hall. Occasionally I was able to rock them to sleep and even comfort them when they cried.

Going from being a homeschooling mom to a full-time working mom was gut-wrenching, especially with two toddlers, but God provided the perfect imperfect situation. That to me was so much more than I had asked or imagined.

> *Now to him who is able to do immeasurably more than all we ask or imagine, according to his power that is at work within us, to him be glory in the church and in Christ Jesus throughout all generations, for ever and ever! Amen.*
>
> —Ephesians 3:20-21

2. *God is worthy of our trust (Psalm 37:5–6; 1 Thessalonians 5:24).* I had a lot of fearful and anxious thoughts based on the reality that was my life. But God was faithful to help me deal with each one. I feared the loss of my husband, and although that did indeed happen, God proved trustworthy in helping me handle my fears. He provided what I needed when I needed it. He gave me a home, a job, friends who helped with my house, men who modeled godly manhood to my children, faithful friends and family who prayed for us daily, and the strength to meet each day.

Implicit in the directive to trust God is a big "do not worry." In Matthew 6 Jesus speaks to this worry many of us struggle with daily. He compares us to birds that "do not sow or reap or store away" food but are fed by our heavenly Father. Jesus asks us, "Are you not much more valuable than they? Who of you by worrying can add a single hour to his life?"

(verses 26–27). Our Father knows what we need, and He will provide (verses 32–33). Beloved, God loves you very much, and He can be trusted with your life.

3. *There is hope (Psalm 25:3; Ephesians 1:18–19).* The mere fact that God has allowed me to write this book is a picture of Him making something beautiful out of something exceedingly difficult. He has a plan for my life, and He has a plan for yours. Jeremiah 29:11 says, " 'For I know the plans I have for you,' declares the LORD, 'plans to prosper you and not to harm you, plans to give you hope and a future.' "

> *Do not let your hearts be troubled. Trust in God; trust also in me.*
>
> —JOHN 14:1

God said those words to the people of Israel while they were still in captivity. God wasn't going to leave them there; He had a plan for them, and it was good. In little ways, I feel hopefulness each time I laugh with my children, each time my children say they love me, and each time they make good decisions. I'm thankful and hopeful because God is allowing me to be part of the redemption of this difficult period in my life and the lives of my children.

MEDIC! DEALING WITH BATTLE WOUNDS AND SCARS

Regardless of whether your marriage ended two days, two months, or two years ago, or whether you're still battling to save your marriage, we share a common experience of grieving our losses. Each of us is somewhere along the continuum of grief: denial, anger, bargaining, depression, and acceptance. Denial, the first stage of grief, is marked by disbelief. We simply can't believe what is happening to us or around us. When we finally grasp the magnitude of the betrayal, blazing anger bursts onto the scene. We feel righteous indignation, which often gives way to bargaining. This is when we try to figure out a way to make things work, to go back to the way life was, or change it for the better.

At some point along the grief continuum, hopelessness and depression might become our daily companions. When these two difficult emotions are dealt with effectively, we can finally reach a point of acceptance and begin looking forward to what the future holds for us. Each of us is coming to grips with both our new reality and the battle scars we got along the way. Understanding how we got here and what it looks like to come to grips with reality in a healthy way is a huge part of being able to move forward and heal.

Someone shared with me that there is an "unnatural natural progression" in the breakup of a family. See if this resonates with you. First, one spouse turns his (or her) back on God and then abandons his partner emotionally, physically, and spiritually. Once he has thrown away his relationships with his Savior and his spouse, it isn't difficult to see that his children easily become the third casualty. I watched that exact process happen in my marriage. I just didn't realize what was happening until it was too late.

There were a few signs of my husband's struggles even during our first year of marriage, but I essentially ignored them. I know that many of my husband's struggles began before he met me. I loved his family—and still do—but adultery was a pervasive theme in their home. My husband's father left his wife when my husband was a young teenager—the same age as our oldest son when my husband left. My husband had always promised me that he wouldn't repeat the sins of his father. When his father left his second wife, my husband wept and emphatically declared he wouldn't do that to me, ever. (Thankfully, my ex-husband's father has since committed his life to Jesus, and he is indeed "a new creation" in Christ [2 Corinthians 5:17].)

The marriage counselor we went to said that all these things in his family played into the struggles my husband faced daily. I can look back now and see many red flags regarding my husband's behavior, including simple interactions I observed between my husband and other women. There was definitely a difference between friendly and flirtatious. I chose most often to believe that my handsome, gregarious husband was just a very friendly man. And he was, but he was a consummate flirt as well. His flirting often made me feel devalued. I did ask at one point that he not flirt in front of me. I should have stated that request as, "Don't flirt with other women, period."

After I read Shaunti Feldhahn's book *For Women Only*, my husband and I had a conversation about the visual struggles men have with regard to women. He said he didn't struggle with this kind of temptation at all. I'd married the only man in the world who didn't struggle with admiring beautiful women! I probably should have recognized that false claim as a warning flag. Really, most of the things that I look back on were relatively insignificant things. But when I put them all together now, they paint a picture I doubtless should have seen more clearly.

After my husband left, I wondered, *Why didn't I pick up on things sooner?* I wish I knew why I didn't acknowledge my gut feelings back then. Why didn't I confront his flirting more directly and with some tenacity? I think I just loved him and trusted him.

At one point during our divorce process, I spent time reading through my journals from our early years together. As I did, it became clear to me that I did indeed have a sense that something was wrong. But the fact was, I wasn't a suspicious, unhappy wife. I had a happy home and a family I loved. We weren't perfect, and my husband's tendencies to pay attention to other women bothered me, but I knew he loved me and I never thought our relationship was in jeopardy.

Had I understood what was at stake, I would have been more willing to ask harder questions and take notice of uncomfortable feelings and thoughts. I wouldn't have allowed myself to deny the possibility of an affair just because it seemed unfathomable. I would have been vigilant and focused in order to protect what I loved. Unfortunately, by the time I began fighting to save my marriage, it was already too late. I didn't realize it at the time, but the battle had already been lost. All my efforts were in vain.

It is a natural inclination when our marriage has been shattered to focus on the past—to relive, dissect, and rehash old hurts. Although this is normal and expected, it isn't advisable for prolonged periods of time. We can look back and try to evaluate what happened for the purpose of healing and changing for the better, but we must be careful not to continue to punish ourselves. It's a useless and harmful exercise to beat ourselves up for ignoring warning signs or being unaware of them. Regardless of missed signs or ignored inklings, we shouldn't dwell on the past beyond learning from it.

BATTLING BITTERNESS

Probably like many of you, I enjoyed my life with my husband. Our marriage wasn't perfect, but I always thought it was pretty good. In fact, on the day my husband left, he stated that 90 percent of our marriage was great. At that moment, some sarcastic thoughts raced through my mind: *Ninety percent? For real? And you're leaving? Good luck finding a marriage that rates 100 percent, especially with an adulteress!*

Yes, I'll admit I felt a little bitter. For those of you who are reading this book on behalf of a devastated friend, all I can say is . . . welcome to the world of adultery! The battle against bitterness was and is fierce, and I've had to fight hard against it. It isn't easy; in fact, it's really, really hard. But it's a very important battle to win.

If I had allowed bitterness to take root, I wouldn't have been able to overcome thousands of other issues and emotions associated with abandonment and divorce. The number of emotions I felt throughout this nightmare was enormous. I had to recognize my emotions as valid and allow myself to feel them with caution, with concern, and with counsel. I wanted no emotion to overcome me and keep me from doing the things I knew I needed to do.

My faith enabled me to focus on something other than how I was feeling. I learned how to rest in the presence of God, trust in the sovereignty of God, and rely on the provision of God. And I desperately needed that provision, because to truly heal, I needed to *forgive*. That was the single most important thing I could do. And, of course, it was also the single most difficult thing to do. (We'll talk more about this important issue in chapter 5.)

There was a surreal, maddening moment when I realized that I was the "victim," and yet I was the only one fighting for my marriage. The injustice of the offended party having to convince the offender to stay was mind-boggling. So often I wanted to yell, "Hey! You should be begging *me* to stay in this marriage. You are such a jerk!" Actually, I probably did say that. Calling my husband a jerk wasn't edifying or encouraging, but it was the truth as I saw it. Still, although I felt that I had every right to sink into the pit of nastiness, it wasn't really where I wanted to be or where God wanted me to be.

Responding in anger might have seemed like my right and even a reasonable response to my situation, but the result was more pain and less healing. I had many occasions to see and regret my natural inclinations. Those were the times when I learned to rely heavily on the Lord for strength to rise above them. I was so thankful that God understood all the things I was feeling, all the ways I wanted to respond, and the mental, emotional, physical, and spiritual struggle of fighting for my marriage. I knew that God was intimately acquainted with betrayal, grief, and loss (Isaiah 53:3–5; John 13:21). He could handle all my tears and rants and offer comfort in response (Psalm 55:22). He calmed my fears (Psalm 34:4). He was the perfect Medic (Psalm 103:3; 1 Peter 2:24), and He never left my side (Hebrews 13:5). He healed my wounded heart even as the battle raged on.

And if you let Him, He will heal yours, too.

Battle Weary but Winning

In the midst of crisis, I had to survive. I had to face each day, especially as I walked my children through the crisis as well. They were used to my red, wet eyes. They probably heard my weeping in the shower or in bed at night. Only occasionally would they come to check on me. In some strange way, I believe it was comforting for them to know that their mother felt the loss just as intensely as they did.

I know my children found comfort in seeing me move forward and smile at times, even while I was wading through deep sadness. To realize that there can be joy in the midst of great sorrow and grief was a valuable life lesson for them. I didn't always handle things perfectly—I still don't. I surely freaked my kids out at times with my range of emotions. I just know that God enabled me to walk through this crisis with a grace that could only have come from Him.

Honestly, I still feel I didn't get a fighting chance to save my marriage. I'd lost the war before I even knew I was in the battle. Yet in the midst of abandonment and divorce, God gave me His perspective, His people, and His peace. He showed me that His way of looking at things would give me hope. He placed people in my life who loved me and my children through their actions, their words, and their prayers. He poured His peace on me as I took each step, believing His faithfulness and trusting His plan. He can do the same for you.

Thank you for letting me walk by your side into the fray. I pray that you will find your voice as you hear mine. Sometimes it feels as though our abandonment and divorce rob us of our voices. We lose our voices as married individuals, our voices to communicate all we feel, our voices to share our view of the past and to clearly express our vision for the future. But as we march boldly forward, we will successfully find our voices again. This battle is painful, but it is not hopeless.

In the chapters that follow, I won't give you trite answers or throw Bible verses at you in the hope that you will be challenged or blessed or even comforted (though Scripture is comforting and I will share some along the way). I know from experience how easily someone's heartfelt words can wound an already fragile heart. Instead, I'll tell you honestly about my own struggles, my battles with negative emotions, my fears, and my failures. We will surely find common ground in those things.

Wait for the LORD;
be strong, and let your
heart take courage;
wait for the LORD!
—PSALM 27:14, ESV

More importantly, I want to share the many ways God has blessed my family in the midst of our pain, how my faith has been strengthened, and how my fear has been replaced with hope. My prayer is that you will find healing as you read through the pages of this book. I have found healing as I've written it. There is strength and hope and healing at the end of this sorrow. We will claim it together.

Lord, Your Word says that You are the "Father of mercies" and the "God of all comfort, who comforts us in all our affliction, so that we may be able to comfort those who are in any affliction" with the comfort we have received from You (2 Corinthians 1:3–4, ESV).

God, sometimes it's so difficult to see beyond our own pain and suffering and to feel any ability to bless or comfort those around us. Lord, despite our own pain, please help us bless others. Let us find our strength in Christ. Lord, hold our hearts. You know intimately the heartbreak of abandonment and betrayal. Father, please heal our hearts, restore our minds, and mend our broken homes (Psalm 147:3).

As temptations come—those we expect and those we don't—please help us lean heavily on You. Please don't let us lose sight of Jesus. Give us strength to not throw away our confidence, "which has a great reward" (Hebrews 10:35, ESV). We are not of those who "shrink back and are destroyed, but of those who have faith and preserve their souls" (verse 39, ESV)!

God, be glorified in our messy lives. Your Word says You give "strength to the weary" and increase "the power of the weak" (Isaiah 40:29). We boldly ask for Your strength. Let our hearts take courage in You (Psalm 112:8).

In Jesus' name, we pray. Amen.

Two

My Husband, the Stranger Among Us

Do not be afraid or discouraged because of this vast army.
For the battle is not yours, but God's. . . . You will not have
to fight this battle. Take up your positions; stand firm and
see the deliverance the LORD will give you, O Judah and
Jerusalem. Do not be afraid; do not be discouraged. Go out
to face them tomorrow, and the LORD will be with you.

—2 CHRONICLES 20:15, 17

In an instant my life became completely foreign to me. Everything changed beginning the day my husband said he was thinking of leaving. The changes continued as the truth was gradually revealed about the nature of his affair, as I fought desperately to save our marriage, and finally, as my husband and I divorced. At each new stage, I was stunned by what was happening. How had we gotten to this dreadful place? How had life become so strange and painful so quickly? I had an awful gaping hole in the pit of my stomach. I couldn't rest. I couldn't eat. I couldn't breathe. I couldn't accept reality. I just existed in this horrible state of pain and bewilderment.

All those clichés I'd heard became real to me. My heart was breaking. I could feel it shattering. I felt alone. I felt incredibly sorrowful. And sometimes I felt furious. The range of emotions was overwhelming.

During this time, I found the most comfort in Scripture. No one else seemed to be able to say anything that would make things better. But God spoke to me through His Word. Verses I had known for years finally made sense or seemed to take on a depth and dimension that spoke volumes to my pain.

I began in the psalms. I'm sure God led me there. The psalmists spoke with such raw emotions. Granted, their circumstances were quite different from mine, but the way they spoke and how they felt connected with me. Some of the outcomes they wished on their enemies were quite graphic, but during my angry period, those passages spoke clearly to me as well. I could certainly relate!

Journal entry: What are all the emotions I feel in the midst of this disaster? Disbelief seems to be the predominant one for me, but is that actually an emotion? I don't know, but I certainly can say I feel it often enough. The others are anger-based, mostly because of the effects of this situation on my children—frustration at not being able to "fix" things, some fear mixed with anxiety, and an ample amount of worry.

O Lord, please forgive me. You have been such a faithful and loving Father to my children and me. Thank You so much that You are more than able to do immeasurably more than all I ask for or can possibly imagine. I am in awe of Your care for us. Lord, I know that You are taking care of us. I know You have a plan. Please don't let me step out of it. "My soul melts away for sorrow; strengthen me according to your word" (Psalm 119:28, ESV)!

Suffering the Insufferable

The psalmists understood the pain and struggle of this life on earth, but they also knew their Savior. They knew they could lay it all out there. That it was okay to cry out to God in anguish, in fear, in anger, because He was their refuge. I was feeling all the same raw emotions, and I definitely didn't like them. As He did with the psalmists, God lovingly allowed me to pour out all the misery of my heartbreak to Him.

I wanted to emulate the faith of the psalmists. I was inspired that after railing against the injustice and horror of this life, after pleading for God to do something about it, after crying out in sorrow and sadness, they could still praise God and place their trust in Him. My own heart echoed their cries: "Why are you cast down, O my soul, and why are you in turmoil within me? Hope in God; for I shall again praise him, my salvation and my God" (Psalm 43:5, ESV).

The psalmists trusted despite their circumstances, because they knew God's character—trustworthy, faithful, and loving. Like the psalmists, I found that God sometimes answered my prayers with a yes and at other times with a no, and I saw Him use both answers for good. I knew I could trust Him with my hurting self, my weary thoughts, and my pained questions.

I knew that God truly understood how I felt. He didn't just feel bad that I was hurting or weep because I was weeping. He understood all that I was feeling—the sense of betrayal, the pain, the confusion, the hopelessness. There was so much comfort in being understood, especially when most people around me were desperately trying to figure out how to understand me and my emotions. I was blessed to find my voice in the psalms. I was that psalmist imploring God for comfort, strength, and help. Those words on the page were the words rattling around in my head. It was comforting to know that the same faithful God who had heard the psalmists' prayers had heard mine, too.

One of the first scriptures I read when things began to fall apart was Psalm 55. I know the passage is long, but please take the time to read it all. For those who have been abandoned by the one they loved, these words are so poignant.

> I say, "Oh, that I had wings like a dove!
>> I would fly away and be at rest;
> yes, I would wander far away;
>> I would lodge in the wilderness;
> I would hurry to find a shelter
>> from the raging wind and tempest." . . .
>
> For it is not an enemy who taunts me—
>> then I could bear it;
> it is not an adversary who deals insolently with me—
>> then I could hide from him.
> But it is you, a man, my equal,
>> my companion, my familiar friend.
> We used to take sweet counsel together;
>> within God's house we walked in the throng. . . .
>
> But I call to God,
>> and the LORD will save me.
> Evening and morning and at noon
>> I utter my complaint and moan,
>> and he hears my voice.
> He redeems my soul in safety

from the battle that I wage,
    for many are arrayed against me.
God will give ear and humble them,
    he who is enthroned from of old,
because they do not change
    and do not fear God.

My companion stretched out his hand against his friends;
    he violated his covenant.
His speech was smooth as butter,
    yet war was in his heart;
his words were softer than oil,
    yet they were drawn swords.

Cast your burden on the LORD,
    and he will sustain you;
he will never permit
    the righteous to be moved.

But you, O God, will cast them down
    into the pit of destruction;
men of blood and treachery
    shall not live out half their days.
But I will trust in you.
    (Psalm 55:6–8, 12-14, 16–23, ESV, emphasis added)

This passage described my situation and my life well. Moaning, anguish, horror, trembling, wishing to fly away, anger, calling on God to destroy and divide, the betrayal of my companion and familiar friend.

But—and this is a big *but*—I called to God. I couldn't call upon family, friends, pastors, or hit men to save me from my situation. I called to the Lord, and He saved me.

I realized that God wasn't sitting up in heaven waiting to see how I would handle this big mess that landed in my living room. God was right in the middle of it, wading through the dirty laundry, the crusty dishes, the spilled cereal, and the tossed game pieces. He was comforting and holding my weeping, exhausted self and my bewildered, frightened, and hurting children. He was helping me—no, not just helping me; He was showing me how to pick up the pieces of my shattered life.

Practically speaking, God obviously wasn't doing my dishes for me or dealing with my sticky counters, but *His presence* gave me strength to face each task, whether tedious or terrifying.

There are particularly difficult times in our lives when we completely understand that God is our strength. We realize that it isn't about coping with a situation; it's about living in God's strength. It's a surprisingly exquisite and painful place to be.

Each morning I would wake up earlier than any human being should. I would tiptoe downstairs, make some tea, light a scented candle, and pull out my Bible. I believed that God had awakened me for these times with Him. And each night I ended the day in His presence, praying for peaceful sleep and new mercies in the morning (Lamentations 3:22–23).

I know that getting up at the crack of dawn to read Scripture and pray may seem far-fetched to some. But many people I have spoken with have experienced healing and renewed focus by spending extensive time in God's Word and in God's presence during times of adversity. As I share how God met me in my desperate places, I'm not trying to set an unattainable goal or standard for you. My heart's desire is to convey that God met my needs and blessed me during my time with Him. And He is more than willing and able to do that for you, too, though how He meets you might look different.

Those times with God were often the sweetest of my day or night. Other activities like watching television or reading books might have distracted me from my heartache, but I wanted more than a diversion. I wanted to tap into the Source of my hope, help, and consolation. To immerse myself in His Word each morning, I did indeed sacrifice sleep, but it was fitful sleep at best, anyway. I did have to focus on Him to the exclusion of other things, but it was the right focus, and it enabled me to do the most important things well.

There are many days now when I wish I could go back to that focused time. It was a time of great peace in the midst of great chaos. My healing wasn't the result of anything I did. It was a direct result of all that God did. It wasn't because I'm exceptional in any way; it was because He is exceptional in every way. If you are brokenhearted right now, I want to encourage you that God can bring you to a place where you feel whole again. He can give you peace in the middle of chaos.

His Word reminded me who I am and whose I am. I am His child, and He was able to take care of my stuff. No matter how difficult life's circumstances became, I could trust Him to give me wisdom to deal with them and strength to persevere. Those early morning quiet times were the first times in my life when I felt truly intimate with God. It made a difference in my day. Everything around me was spiraling out of control, or at least looked that way, but after absorbing God's Word, I was able to experience calm and peace.

FAMILIAR FEELINGS IN THE UNFAMILIAR

In the weeks leading up to my husband's departure, I tried to do everything I could to convince him to stay. I wrote love letters reminding him of our past eighteen years together. I organized, decluttered, and beautified our home. I made his favorite meals, didn't bother him at work, and offered to take up running with him. I reminded him again and again of our precious children, our friendship, and our love for one another. I did "The Love Dare" challenge. (Maybe I should ask for a refund!)

I asked him, "If you would give up your life for your children, why not give up your mistress?" Did he not understand the ramifications his leaving would have on our children? Weren't we happy? I begged him for a reason for why he was doing this. The only reason he ever gave was that I always wanted him home from work on time. Ironically, that wasn't the truth. I couldn't win for losing on that one.

I remember weeping on his shoulder after a particularly difficult day with our children. I pleaded with him not to leave me as a single mom of five children. I begged him to give us another chance. I offered to move anywhere, do anything, never mention this to anyone, have breast-enhancement surgery, stop homeschooling, go to work, anything! I was desperate.

Only God's grace and love enabled me to pursue my husband. I loved him even when it was nearly impossible to do so. But oh how I struggled not to rail against him or voice my opinion of his actions. It took great self-restraint to keep my mouth shut and not try to be the Holy Spirit. I tried to look to the future and see what awesome things could happen if we were reconciled. I had it all worked out. It was going to be amazing! The testimony we would have for others struggling in their marriages. The strength we could nurture by surviving this. The intimacy we could experience by being willing to share all our struggles rather than walking through minefields alone. I just knew we were going to be stronger and better because of this trial. And we were going to be more in love than ever.

Of course, the hard truth is that none of those things happened. The more I pursued my husband, the more I loved him, and the more I tried, the faster he ran, the meaner he became, and the less he cared. I was "heap[ing] burning coals on his head" (Proverbs 25:22). My kindness in the face of his betrayal was making him withdraw even more.

Although I believe he felt guilty on some level, he wouldn't stop seeing the other woman. He refused to put any boundaries on their relationship. It seemed that I was the only one fighting for our marriage. After weeks of going to marriage counseling and even attending a FamilyLife marriage conference together, my husband seemed even more distant. During the marriage conference, he refused to participate in any of the activities with me. He wouldn't hold me, kiss me, or make love to me either. He implied that he felt he would be cheating on her. Obviously, he wasn't planning to renew his vows at the end of the conference.

Our trip home was a nightmare (as if our life wasn't a nightmare already). My husband was like a robot—unemotional, detached, and indifferent. I was a mess—emotional, frantic, and desperate. When we arrived home, he took his journal and Bible and told me he needed to go process everything. I called my dear friend Mary and asked her to pray hard. I hoped the words of wisdom we'd heard at the conference had made some sort of positive impression. I wanted to remind him of the speaker's words that if the grass was greener on the other side of the fence, it was being fed by a sewage tank.

Unfortunately, not too much later, Mary and her husband, Kevin, called with terrible news. While driving our sons to football practice for us, they had seen my husband pull into his mistress's neighborhood. They quickly dropped off the boys, and Kevin followed him. When he found her house and knocked on the front door, there was no answer. Kevin called our pastor, who immediately headed over to the house.

Together they stood in her yard, calling my husband's cell phone and trying to convince him to come outside. My husband remained inside with his mistress. Eventually after over an hour of trying, our pastor and Kevin left and headed to my house. It was like a bad soap opera with a particularly awful ending. It took hours for my husband to return home. He sat on the sofa and didn't blink an eye as our dearest friends and pastor confronted him. I couldn't think of a thing to say. I was in shock.

When everyone left, he finally showed some emotion: anger. He was angry that anyone would question him. I told him I was sorry he felt that way. Pathetic, I know. I just wanted so badly for him to choose me. That night I lay next to my husband and wept quietly, prayed silently, and hurt deeply.

The following night we sat on our sofa and had the only entirely honest conversation of this whole ordeal. He shared all about his relationship with her and how he felt about her. He shared about their e-mails, texts, games, signals, and inside jokes. He told me if he had met her first, he would have chosen her.

Hours into our conversation, he looked at me in astonishment and thanked me for listening. He said he never dreamed I would be so understanding and loving. Me, either. It was literally the most difficult and painful conversation I've ever had to participate in. I know it doesn't make sense, but the fact that he was finally coming clean and being honest gave me hope. But it was a false hope, because at no time did he stop communicating with her.

To me, the obvious choice was our family. I couldn't comprehend how he wasn't seeing that. I couldn't understand why God wasn't changing his heart and mind. I implored God to take his affection for her away. Then I asked God to change her heart and open her eyes to the pain their affair was causing. As far as I could see, those prayers weren't being answered in the way I hoped. My husband's behavior at home became more and more difficult to deal with kindly.

He was terse with our children—impatient and annoyed by any

childlike behavior. My children were hurting and bewildered, and I couldn't stand what was happening to our family. I was so frustrated that no matter how hard I tried to fix things, I couldn't. I was running out of options. All my friends who knew of the situation had differing opinions and advice. I was beyond confused.

I got to the point where I realized that I didn't know how to fix it. "Fixing it" was a God-sized task. I was terrified I'd do something wrong and make it all worse, if that were even possible. What if I forced him to stay with me, and he just continued having affairs? What if I let him go and lost him forever? What if I filed for divorce and ruined any hope of reconciliation? What if he seemed repentant and I took him back only to have this happen again in a couple of years? What if . . . what if . . . what if? As my head spun with questions, I realized once again that the Lord was my only hope. I couldn't see the big picture, but God did.

Separating the Inseparable

I desperately wanted to stay in God's will. It wasn't that I was this amazingly godly woman. I just felt so convinced that the only way anything was going to work out was by my being smack-dab in the middle of God's will. I pursued His will with a passion. I spoke with my pastor. I sought the advice of our marriage counselor. I listened to the advice of my friends. I prayed. Though it wasn't easy, I *chose* to trust that God would lead me, and He did.

After many weeks of hoping and trying to save my marriage with no positive results, I was counseled that it was time to force my husband to make a decision. At first I balked. I didn't want to chance driving him away. Many suggested that maybe this would wake him up. It seemed a risky move. Was I willing to abide by my ultimatum if it didn't go the way I hoped? I had to decide. I went back to my knees and my Bible.

I read verse after verse about the battle being the Lord's (2 Chronicles 20:15). I was reminded that God could use anything for His purposes. A friend pointed out to me that although my husband was physically in our home, his heart had left. Another friend told me that I could always take him back if he chose to leave. I realized that saying "choose" didn't mean I was saying "leave."

The night I chose to give my husband the ultimatum was one of the saddest of my life. My counselor advised me to have a separation agreement ready for him to sign before he left the house. So I prepared for the meeting with a hastily written separation agreement in one hand and a Bible in the other. I spent the hours before his arrival praying, reading psalms, and asking that God make it very clear if this was His will. He did.

My husband arrived home late; I suspected that he had been running with her. He didn't notice the absence of our five children, who were hanging out at the home of some of my dear friends. This was inconceivable to me. He was rude, demanding, and arrogant—behaviors he had rarely exhibited prior to revealing his affair. I prepared dinner and sat with him while he ate. I had no appetite. After dinner I asked if we could talk. He agreed.

I stated, "You need to make a decision tonight. Are you going to stay with me and our children, or are you going to go with her?" As I asked, I slid the separation agreement across the table. I said that if he decided to leave, which I so hoped he wouldn't, that I needed him to sign this piece of paper. I needed to know that he would still provide for the children and me. He put his hand on it and pulled it toward him. It was a simple act, but I knew it signified much more.

As we sat there reading through the document together, I couldn't believe that only a few months prior to this, we were happily celebrating our seventeenth wedding anniversary. Mere weeks before, he had given me a gorgeous necklace, my favorite perfume, and a lovely card inscribed with his handwritten sentiments of how much he loved me. What in the world had happened? How could he throw our friendship, our love, our marriage, and our family away so easily?

This one sheet of paper was going to define our future, and he was sitting there making slight changes, initialing things as if we were buying a dishwasher. I don't think, at that point, I had any emotions—unless shock is considered an emotion. After he signed the agreement, he stood up and said he needed to collect some things. He told me he was going to stay at his office, which I discovered later was a lie. I packed him snacks and drinks and got him a pillow and a sleeping bag. I was such a fool.

As he stood at our front door preparing to leave, I wept uncontrollably. He held me briefly and said, "I don't know if this is me leaving forever or the start of me coming home." I thought, *What does that mean?* I didn't understand it then and I still don't. I found out later that he went straight to her house. He left forever.

I guess it should have come as no surprise that he left. He had given no indication that he was willing to truly work on our marriage. Still, I had hoped that something would stir in his heart, and he would realize that we were worth it. I didn't think that we would eventually divorce. I thought this might actually bring some reality to his life. That maybe the fairy-tale world he was living in would end, and he would come back.

The counselor said that he was idealizing the other woman and was dismissing me. I hoped she would be horrible to live with and have nasty PMS symptoms—apparently not. My ultimatum wasn't a request for divorce. I was merely allowing him to experience consequences for his actions. Unfortunately, the consequences didn't deter him from his destructive course of action.

Although I had lost this first battle for my marriage, I hadn't given up. I was determined to continue fighting for my husband. I wouldn't accept that things were hopeless. I wouldn't give up until God showed me very clearly that I should. I believed that God could do anything, and I believed that the man I had married was hidden somewhere inside this stranger.

ACCEPTING THE UNACCEPTABLE

I distinctly remember the first time I saw my husband after he moved out. He looked awful—at least that was my impression. Maybe it was just wishful thinking. He was skinny and disheveled and stood with slouched shoulders. I thought he looked defeated and unhappy. The thing that struck me was that he smelled different. You know how our homes each have specific scents? His scent was no longer ours; it was hers. And, frankly, he didn't smell good to me. Maybe this change was one of God's mercies to me. There is nothing attractive about sin.

Each encounter with my husband consisted of my trying desperately to remind myself that this man I had known intimately for so many years wasn't who I thought he was. I had to convince myself that I couldn't trust him. I could no longer treat him as my companion and friend. Those terms didn't apply at all. He had, in fact, become a kind of enemy. I was in a battle for the security and provision of my children. He was my adversary, and I hated it. I struggled to convince myself of this fact. I just wanted to make up and be friends . . . Actually, I wanted my husband back. But he wouldn't cooperate. He wouldn't participate in a logical conversation. He wouldn't engage with our children. He wouldn't try to restore our marriage. He wouldn't give up his mistress. Yet I fought on.

There are a thousand words I could use to describe my life at that time—words like *unjust, unfair, selfish, ridiculous, pathetic, juvenile, frustrating*. My husband had done all that was awful to do to a wife and his children and acted as though he still expected kindness and respect. And honestly, it was difficult not to fall back into old patterns of relating. I still wanted to take care of him and do things for him. If he was picking up the children, I would make him a plate of dinner. He never thanked me. Ugh! I felt like a dog going back to get another kick. Everything was so confusing. I couldn't get my emotions to line up with reality.

There were even times when I longed for him to hold me, all while he was betraying me. For seventeen years he had been my husband, comforter, and friend. I couldn't wrap my brain around the change in our relationship and circumstances. I loved him. It was difficult to forget those feelings.

I had to consciously set boundaries to protect my heart and my mind. I stopped having contact with him when he was picking up the children. I tried to minimize our conversations and instead chose to communicate through e-mail. This took the emotions out of the equation. It helped. Eventually I was able to get my heart, head, and reality to line up.

I accepted the fact that my husband was a different person now. It became impossible to fool myself into believing this was the same man I had married when each interaction proved otherwise. The man I knew, loved, married, and had made and adopted babies with was no longer evident. I can honestly say that I hope that somewhere deep inside him is the kind, loving, and fun man I once knew, and that someday he will reappear.

This place of acceptance didn't come easily. It took time and it was hard fought. I didn't want to accept the reality that my husband didn't act, think, or feel the same way he had before. It sounds odd to say that I struggled with showing him kindness after I shared earlier that I struggled with being too kind to him. There was a war being waged within me.

One side of me wanted desperately for things to be the way they were when we were happily married. That side was willing to overlook a lot and put aside the pain. The other side of me was very much aware of the crushing sorrow and terrible betrayal. That side wrestled with showing my husband any consideration and, at times, grappled with negative feelings toward anyone who was even civil to him.

After he moved in with his mistress and stepped out of our lives in every way, the aware side of me began to win the war. I didn't want anyone to be kind to him or even say hi to him. If he attended one of our children's sporting events, I wanted to plaster scarlet letter *A*s all over his body. I wanted everyone to know what awful things he had done. Though I held back from doing so, I really wanted to share my side whenever and however I could.

I believe I was in three stages of grief simultaneously—denial, anger, and bargaining. I think that's the way it is with grief sometimes. It's easy to get spun around a bit as emotions fluctuate and wounds are reopened. It most certainly is a wild, nauseating ride. Getting off the ride was only possible when I began to understand and accept not only what had happened but also that my husband had changed dramatically—and not for the better.

I had to learn to live and function within the new paradigm of our relationship. I had to accept reality, and that meant there would be difficult days when I would struggle with anger and sad days when I would be willing to do anything to make things "all better."

Acceptance didn't mean there would no longer be sorrow or pain. It also didn't mean I gave up on fighting for my marriage or, as divorce became imminent, fighting for my children and our security. It just gave me the strength to move forward.

Bearing the Unbearable

The first several months after my husband left were awful and amazing all at the same time. His departure made my very private fight for our marriage quite public. Seriously public. My husband held a high-profile public-official job in our city. He was having an affair with one of his employees. Within a week it was front-page news, and a week after that he was fired, very publicly. It was mentioned on almost every TV and radio station in our state. It was written about in almost every newspaper, including the *Washington Post*.

It was surreal. We were just this little family in a little city—why should anyone care about our family shattering? Did anyone *really* care? I'll tell you how God answered that query: Friends cared. They jumped into my life in ways I couldn't even imagine. I had a support system that was unbelievable. My children saw the body of Christ come together and love them in very tangible ways.

Each night, after I rocked my little ones and read to my big ones, and they were all fast asleep, I'd sit on the sofa and saturate myself with Scripture. I couldn't get enough of it. It became my lifeline. I would weep and pray and weep and read and weep and write. I was truly like a deer panting for water. I was desperate for wisdom, strength, and peace, and God provided it all in His Word.

> *An anxious heart weighs a man down, but a kind word cheers him up.*
>
> —PROVERBS 12:25

As I struggled to find my balance and make life-altering decisions in the midst of this crisis, I had to keep my eyes focused with laser intensity on my Savior. If I focused too much on my circumstances, I felt overcome with fear and sorrow. On the other hand, if I made Christ my focal point, I had an inexplicable calm, even with a broken heart.

When I felt the weakest, there always seemed to be a reservoir of strength available to help me carry on. I'd often wondered what God meant when He spoke of His strength being ours. I discovered that it meant when things looked darkest, I still had hope. When things felt hopeless, I still had peace. When things seemed too sorrowful to bear, I could find joy in the anticipation of what God was going to do. When I was afraid, His faithfulness gave me courage.

His words also encouraged me to fight my fear and anxious thoughts. Not a day went by that I didn't struggle with anxiety and fear. I was afraid of losing my husband, of raising my children alone, of being a single parent, of being single, period. I was afraid I wouldn't be able to provide for my children, that we would be homeless and hungry. I was afraid that people wouldn't believe my account of what had happened. I was afraid I would no longer have any kind of valuable Christian testimony. How wrong I was! God provided financial security, friends who believed me and believed in me, and a testimony that was only strengthened by this adversity.

His words filled me with hope. Jeremiah 17:7–8 says,

> Blessed is the man who trusts in the LORD,
>   whose confidence is in him.
> He will be like a tree planted by the water. . . .
> It does not fear when heat comes;
>   its leaves are always green.
> It has no worries in a year of drought
>   and never fails to bear fruit.

That tree bore fruit regardless of its circumstances. Though a big drought had definitely hit my world and the heat was persistent, like that tree, I didn't need to worry, because God had a good plan for my life.

THE BATTLE BELONGS TO THE LORD

Whatever God calls you to do in your situation, know that He will walk you through it. He will "never leave you nor forsake you" (Deuteronomy 31:6; Joshua 1:5; see Hebrews 13:5). What you're going through is tough and challenging and heartbreaking, but you have to keep following God's leading. This isn't simply a battle for your marriage or your emotional survival; it's a spiritual battle as well. That sounds spooky, but let me explain. The Bible tells us, "For our struggle is not against flesh and blood, but against the rulers, against the authorities, against the powers of this dark world and against the spiritual forces of evil in the heavenly realms" (Ephesians 6:12).

God has given you instructions for how to deal with spiritual warfare. And He has armor for you to put on—truth, righteousness, the gospel of peace, faith, salvation, and the Word of God (Ephesians 6:13–17). Each of these is invaluable in the fight to stand firm during difficult times. Knowing the truth of who God is and how deeply He loves you is foundational to your success.

Putting on the righteousness offered through Christ gives you the ability to live in a way that testifies to God's work in your life. Your worth is not measured by your abilities, successes, or failures. It is totally and completely based on who you are in Christ. If you are a believer, Christ's righteousness is yours. And it is His righteousness that enables you to live your life free from guilt and fear.

Sharing the gospel of peace with yourself and others daily is strengthening; it reminds you of your sweet Savior, who loves you. One of the most practical ways to apply this is by sharing with your children how God has provided for you or cared for your family; in this way you are pointing out things that inspire and strengthen your children's faith, as well as your own.

Faith gives you hope for the present and the future. Your faith enables you to overcome the struggles you are going through. The same power that God used to create the world, the universe, and us is the same power He uses in your life! For me, I can't comprehend it but I'm grateful for it!

Your salvation through Christ helps you maintain the perspective that sin can't play mind games with you; you are no longer a slave to sin.

Remember that it's not about what you do or what you've done; your salvation is based on what Christ has already done for you.

Finally, the Word of God is your sword—it is your only offensive weapon. You can use the Word of God to fight the fears that assail you, the temptations that try you, and the overwhelming emotions that you carry around. That means you know Scripture so well that you have peace despite your circumstances (Philippians 4:6–7). Maybe it means that the words coming out of your mouth, even under duress, are gentle. Maybe it means that you have an answer for what you believe, even when your circumstances are beyond difficult (Colossians 4:6).

You must base your answers not on what you're feeling but rather on what you know to be true—what you believe. You must keep your eyes focused on the Lord and be ready to do what He leads you to do to win this battle—whether it looks like the victory you hoped for or the victory God has designed for you. The only way to do this is to be covered in God's armor. Remember, He has not just equipped you for battle; He has equipped you for victory.

Don't give up! Let God be part of your journey, and He will pour His peace into your heart and mind. He will give you strength to face each day. He will help you speak well for yourself and your children. He will guide you each day. He will fight this battle for you!

Father, we pray that our "love may abound more and more in knowledge and depth of insight," so that we may "discern what is best and may be pure and blameless until the day of Christ, filled with the fruit of righteousness that comes through Jesus Christ—to the glory and praise of God" (Philippians 1:9–11).

God, it is so difficult to walk this path without looking down. We have so much to think about, so much to decide, so many things to deal with. Lord, help us to keep our eyes fixed on Jesus. Please, Lord, grant us Your peace, "which surpasses all understanding" (Philippians 4:6–7, esv). Help us "give thanks in all circumstances," even when our world is crashing down around us (1 Thessalonians 5:18). You say the battle is Yours, Lord—please fight for us. Help us to live as "more than conquerors," and through our lives may others be blessed (see 2 Chronicles 20:15; Romans 8:37).

In Jesus' name, amen.

THREE

I Don't Want to Play with a Cheater

When I thought how to understand this, it seemed to me a wearisome task, until I went into the sanctuary of God.

—PSALM 73:16–17, ESV

After praying and pleading with God for a miracle, I finally accepted that my husband wasn't coming back. At that point, I had to make some pretty serious decisions. For example, as a Christian woman, was it okay to be the one who filed for divorce? My case was pretty cut and dried. It helped that my husband announced to the world via newspaper, radio, and TV that he was an adulterer. Okay, maybe it wasn't exactly his choice to come clean publicly, but leaving his family and moving in with another woman was most certainly his choice.

Legally, that made things straightforward, to say the least—spiritually, too. I believed I was scripturally within my right to divorce my husband (Matthew 5:31–32). But I had to decide if that was what God wanted me to do in this circumstance. Could I still live as the Christian woman I wanted to be and divorce my husband?

My decision to file for divorce wasn't because I had given up trying to convince my husband to come home, nor was it because I was angry and wanted out. I decided to file because legally it was the right thing to do to protect my children and myself from further harm. Unfortunately, in the world we live in, we have to think along the lines of legalities and financial security. I truly wrestled with this way of thinking because I didn't want to appear as if I didn't trust God with my family's future and security.

But in the end, I realized that God had put a godly attorney in my life to protect my family. She wanted reconciliation almost as badly as I did, and she hoped and prayed with me for a miracle. She was also my reality check. When I was emotionally spent, she fought on. When I was confused, she explained. When I was afraid, she encouraged. When I was crying, she cried with me. When I needed to vent, she made me laugh through it. I was so very thankful for her role in my life and for her friendship.

My attorney kept reminding me that divorce didn't mean there was no hope. She said that the process could be stopped at any point for reconciliation, and that even after divorce, my husband and I could always remarry. Many people I consulted thought that my filing for divorce would be the wake-up call my husband needed. I remained hopeful that God could and would still work a miracle.

My attorney also reminded me that it was my husband's responsibility to take care of his wife and children, even though he had decided to leave. And in the state where I lived, there were certain things I needed to do to ensure that happened. I had to file the separation agreement, which began the process of divorce whether I liked it or not. I still praise God that He put people in my life who were willing to think beyond my heartache and give me sound advice. Had I not taken that advice, I wouldn't be where I am today. I'm certain my circumstances would be quite different—in the worst possible way.

My husband was very upset when I gave the separation agreement to my attorney for filing to make it a legally binding agreement. Not because it was the beginning of the legal ending of our marriage, but because of the financial repercussions he would suffer. He contended that I bamboozled him into giving away too much, but that was never my intention.

I think sin can blind people to the obvious, make their reasoning senseless, and cause them to frantically search for excuses and someone else to blame for their actions. The night my husband signed that separation agreement, he still expressed a measure of guilt about leaving and was more willing to take care of his family well. My counselor had told me that was how it would be.

He also said that over time, my husband would become less and less generous as he got further and further away from his family and any

Journal entry: Lord, I tried to talk to him, and I just don't understand how his heart has become so hard toward me. Please help me to know what to do. I feel an urgency to get the upper hand legally, but I don't know if that is from You. Please help me do the right thing. Father, I want so desperately to stay in Your will. Please forgive me for talking so much and crying so much.

O Lord, please help me. I'm weary of this, although I think I could hold out longer. I just don't know if that's the right thing to do. I desperately want my husband back, and I desperately want to start the process of healing. Please, Father, please direct my heart and thoughts to what You would have me do. Lord, I pray I would not utter one word outside of Your will. I can tell he has closed his heart to me and to our children. Please help me know how to appropriately address these issues. Please protect and provide for the children and me.

sense of shame. Boy was that true. Thankfully, that hastily written separation agreement, signed on that most dreadful night, provided the foundation for all other agreements and served as my protection during all the negotiations that followed.

When the separation agreement was filed, my husband received notice of the filing. He contacted me and asked if we could pursue divorce without legal counsel. I wasn't comfortable with that arrangement. He had already proved that he was capable of lying and cheating, and it didn't seem wise to move forward without someone representing me. I was still an emotional wreck at times and probably would have failed miserably at negotiating. I still wanted my husband back, so the thought of fighting with him about household items and finances was devastating. I also believed that having someone who wasn't emotionally involved in the situation would be helpful while dealing with the divorce negotiations.

If you have an attorney who isn't a Christian, fear not. God can use anyone to do His will. And there may be times when you don't see eye to eye. My attorney and I didn't always agree on things. I had to learn to trust her wise counsel and also stand up for the things that I felt God was leading me to do. She had an astonishing track record of being right in her advice, but she wasn't God. Ultimately, God was the One I was going to listen to the most attentively.

Thankfully, she and I didn't disagree much. When we did, it was more my denial of the reality of my situation that caused me to drag my feet sometimes regarding her advice. If you don't have an attorney who understands your Christian perspective, be sure to share openly and honestly with him or her exactly what you feel led to do. Listen to your attorney's advice. Pray about it. Seek godly counsel. And then make your decision. Your attorney should support you unless you're making nutty decisions, such as signing over everything in the hope of winning back your spouse's affections. Your attorney works for you and your best interests. And part of that best-interest thing is listening and understanding your desires as both a client and a Christian.

LET THE GAMES BEGIN

Let me say up front that I loathed this divorce game. It was definitely my least favorite game of all time. In fact, going through the divorce was one of the few times in my life when I felt like labeling myself a quitter, taking my ball, and heading home. But I knew if I didn't play well, I wouldn't have a home to go home to!

Divorce is never pretty. Nor is it ever uncomplicated, simple, or easy. It is difficult, time consuming, and painful—not to mention emotionally, physically, and mentally exhausting. Divorce isn't a solution; it's just another problem on top of a problem. Sadly, sometimes it's the only appropriate course of action. I had the support of my church and my family and friends, but that didn't make it easier or less painful.

Unfortunately, I know that support isn't always evident when someone is going through divorce. If you're facing divorce and don't have a solid support system, I encourage you to seek out a Christian counselor or a local support group like DivorceCare. It's important to have people in your life who encourage and support you spiritually, emotionally, mentally, and physically. You need validation that what you're feeling isn't insane. Please find someone who will listen to you and encourage you. Divorce is a painful, heartbreaking crisis, and you need to know that you are not alone, because you truly are *not* alone.

There are moments in divorce when the games are too painful to bear, and no matter how many people are on your team, you just feel devastated. The day I read my husband's first divorce-settlement proposal, my heart broke into a million pieces, and all the daggers in my back twisted a bit more. His characterizations of me and of the night he left were so false and hurtful. I knew that it really shouldn't matter—oh, but it did. He contended that I had tricked him into signing the separation agreement. He stated that I had lied to him about the document by saying that it wasn't legally binding. He was accusing me of being a liar and a cheat, both of which were untrue. He had already chosen another woman to live with, be with, and share his life with; what he thought about me should have been irrelevant. But it's so difficult to change more than seventeen years of relating in the span of a few short months.

His opinion of me had always been the most important to me. Now his opinion was clouded by his desire to paint himself in a better light. I had to be careful not to cloud *my* opinion of me by his words and actions. I needed to remind myself of the truth of who I was and what had happened. Another perfect time to get my head in the Word and my heart focused on Christ. My identity was and is with Christ. I had to remember that no man defined me, either good or bad.

The divorce game isn't ever going to be a slam dunk. It's more like a terribly difficult, swelteringly hot, rocky-road marathon. But you can get through this because it's what you have to do. You can trust that you have a God who loves you and friends and family who care.

Punting with a Purpose

Whether you chose this path or were dragged down it kicking and screaming, you can and will survive. Finding those things that give you strength, direction, and hope can change this marathon of misery into a victory lap in your personal growth.

There are so many things to think about during the divorce process, it's easy to get overwhelmed. Divorce can be life consuming if you let it be. But don't let it consume you. Allow God to make you into the person you were meant to be through, in spite of, and because of this process.

Following are some simple steps I took to help me survive my divorce. No doubt many will seem like no-brainers, but it's so easy to forget the simplest things during divorce. These seven steps are necessary lifelines for anyone struggling through this painful and confusing process.

1. *Find healthy support and trustworthy advisors.* It would have been nearly impossible to survive this whole awful thing without friends who were willing to listen to me share my daily struggles and decision-making issues. These friends were the ones I went to for advice and wise counsel. Finding people who are willing to hear all the sordid details of a divorce for no good reason is quite easy. But it was important that I only share with people who were honorable in their desire to hear and help.

I chose those counselors carefully. I sought advice only from people I knew would pray before answering, were serious about living godly lives, and had some measure of understanding of adversity. I still occasionally saw my counselor, but he felt I had good friends who could help me without charge. My friends didn't shy away from slogging through the mud with me. It was very helpful to be able to thrash out the details and dilemmas of custody, visitation, finances, and possessions with people who truly cared.

Just a bit of advice to consider: If you have children (including teenagers), please protect them by refraining from sharing any more with them than absolutely necessary. Children don't need to know the details, no matter how benign you feel they are. Big-people issues should remain big-people issues.

2. *Guard your tongue.* I believe that we also need to pray that God will enable us to guard our tongues. It's easy to speak harshly when we've been hurt. But it does no good to spew venomous thoughts about our ex-spouses. During my divorce, I'd catch myself being very snarky about my husband. I would often share some sarcastic, scathing comment under the guise of using humor to cope with my situation. But there came a

time when I realized that my heart had changed before my mouth had. My cutting comments no longer reflected the state of my heart. They had just become a habit, my stand-up routine. So I started being more careful with my words, and friends commented on how much happier and peaceful I seemed. It took a lot of self-control to keep my tongue regulated, but ultimately it helped me heal.

3. *Put your children's needs at the top of the list.* When I was struggling to figure things out and was having innumerable conversations with friends, family, and attorneys, it was easy for my children to feel neglected. At one point I caught myself spending way too much time sharing with friends and way too little time being with my children. It was important that they know they were my priority, and I was available to them whenever and wherever they needed me. I determined that all my phone conversations would occur when they were either asleep or not with me. This enabled me not only to focus on my children more, but also to have conversations without fear of little ears overhearing me.

It's helpful to make time for your children as individuals as well as en masse. Each of my children needed different kinds of attention and encouragement from me. (We'll talk about this further in chapter 4.) They also needed just plain old fun time with Mom. I carved out time every day to love on each of my children, even if it was simply a hug, a short catch-up conversation, or a snuggle at bedtime.

I know that when your world is crashing in on you, the thought of making time for anything more than survival is daunting, but you and your children need these little times of blessing throughout each week.

4. *Build a home full of grace.* My priorities changed significantly when my husband left. I didn't spend as much time worrying about sticky floors or dusty pianos. The people in my home became my priority. I learned to be patient when my kids struggled with things. I watched for signs of anger, hurt, or misunderstanding and tried to deal with them compas-

sionately. I sought to offer grace whenever possible. I absolutely needed a lot of grace thrown my way as well. I was working with a significantly diminished emotional reservoir and could often be less than patient and kind, but my heart was set on loving my children well and providing them with a grace-filled home where we could heal.

We needed some time to feel like ourselves again, to understand our new normal. We spent much more time together just enjoying each other's company. We played board games, sweated through basketball games in the driveway, and hiked the parks in our hometown. Due to financial constraints, we didn't participate in the things we had in the past. We lived a very simple life, and it was just wonderful. I believe it was God's way of giving me the right focus and perspective. I put aside my past worries about a stunning home and a busy, productive life and replaced them with time focused on my beautiful children and a peaceful life.

5. Seek referrals for an attorney. It's helpful to ask people you trust to recommend a good attorney. I found a friend to represent me, which worked very well for me but might not be ideal for everyone. If you have a friend who has gone through a divorce, or you attend a divorce support group, ask for their advice. If your church or a church near you has a DivorceCare program, you might seek out the leader and ask for recommendations.

It's important to find an attorney who will not only represent you well but will also present your case in a way you feel comfortable with. If the most important thing to you is that you and your spouse remain civil, you'll want an attorney who is willing to facilitate that attitude throughout the process. If you want to ensure that you and your children are well provided for, no matter what your relationship with your ex happens to be, then it's important to find an attorney who will assertively and ethically advocate for your needs. But above all, it's essential to find an attorney who plays fair—wise but fair.

6. Find the strength to continue when you want to give up. There were so many important, life-changing decisions to make during my divorce. It's exhausting just recalling the process. I couldn't have walked this path alone. I know I would have given up. There were many times when I was just plain done. I desperately wanted to quit. I was often heard saying, "Done! Didn't want to do this in the first place. He can figure out how to do this without me. I don't care anymore."

I cared, but I just wanted to focus on getting my children through the crisis. I didn't have time for all the ridiculousness. Whenever I wanted to throw in the towel, my friends and family gently got my head back in the game and encouraged me to keep going. Divorce is an exhausting and awful process, but it will end. When you feel worn down and ready to give up, look to the Lord, as well as family and friends, for the hope and strength to keep going.

7. Make time for yourself. There wasn't time to hide away while I was fighting for my marriage and dealing with divorce negotiations. Although God definitely provided rest for my soul when I was reading my Bible and praying, I had to find other activities that offered me a respite from the drama and allowed me to relax and maybe even reenergize.

I found that journaling, playing the piano, chatting with friends, exercising, and playing with my children were the most helpful things. I also considered joining a dodgeball league at a local sports complex. The idea of aggressively throwing a ball was mighty appealing at the time! I'm just sayin'!

It's also important to stay as healthy as you can. There will be days when you're so distraught that you have no appetite. I've been there. Try to be intentional about eating healthful foods and staying hydrated to stay physically strong.

And, of course, please make a serious effort to get some sleep. I was less successful at this than I care to admit. There were days when it was difficult to stop the racing thoughts, and then there were other days I could barely keep my eyes open enough to make school lunches. It's important to find balance in your life. Set a bedtime and try to stick with it—a reasonable bedtime. Find time to quiet your mind at the end of the day. You could read something lighthearted, take a bubble bath, listen to some calming music, or journal to get all your thoughts out. Sleep is vital to your mental, emotional, and physical health.

You can do this! You can survive divorce and find yourself stronger and wiser at the end. Please don't get lost in the battle! Find time to get the encouragement, support, and rest you need.

Playing by the Rules

So, what were the rules of this divorce game? Or were there any rules at all? Maybe the overriding rule was *every man for himself*. (Or in my case, every woman for herself!) The whole horrible process went against everything I was raised to be. I didn't want to be mean, selfish, sneaky, manipulative, or difficult. Throughout the legal proceedings, I felt as if I was all those things at one point or another.

I felt mean to be holding firmly to what we had agreed to the evening my husband left. It could have been construed as harsh, but he had initialed and signed the separation agreement, and it took care of my children and me well. I felt selfish when I realized what his portion would be, but I had five children to keep in mind. I felt sneaky as I kept lists of his actions or recorded conversations. I felt manipulative as I tried to figure out a good initial offer so I'd get what I wanted in the end. I felt difficult when I had to hold firm to our final agreement when it was almost punitive to him. But trust me when I tell you that the needs of five children can be expensive.

I was trying so hard to be a godly woman in the midst of this trial.

I wanted to respond to things without bitterness and anger. I wanted to be honest in all my dealings with my husband. I didn't want to be manipulative or difficult just to be difficult. In a strange sort of way, I wanted to treat him respectfully because he was still my husband. Boy was that tough! I tried to think of ways to respond to him in a Christlike manner. I know I didn't always rise to the occasion. I just really didn't want to play games with this person I had loved, trusted, and relied upon for so many years.

As my attorney warned me about my husband's potential responses, I would invariably say, "No, he wouldn't do that!" But then, dang it, he pretty much always did! At first I couldn't believe it; then I couldn't understand it; then I would just get plain old angry about it. Anger never served me well, except to push me to fight for what was right with more diligence and less whining.

I have so many memories of pacing in my backyard, trying to figure out the best agreement we could make. My attorney would try to explain things like alimony versus child support and retirement accounts and pensions, as well as all the things my husband could do to make my life difficult. My head was spinning half the time—no, definitely more than half the time.

As I was wandering back and forth in my yard, I had five hurting little people inside whom I desperately wanted to hold, comfort, and love on. It frustrated me that the whole divorce process took away time I could have been spending with them. To be honest, there were moments when it felt like a big waste of time. I know it wasn't, but it sure *felt* that way. It was necessary to be wise in my dealings with my husband. It was imperative that I not give up just because it was unpleasant. I had to think and not just feel. It was important to think about the future—both mine and my children's—so that we could be in the best possible position to heal and survive.

I needed to approach all the legal issues with wisdom and strength. It wasn't something anyone could do for me. I had to accept and consider the reality of all the eventualities we were discussing. Could I support my children with a certain amount of money? What about the value of all my years as a stay-at-home/homeschooling mom with regard to retirement? I couldn't approach this divorce process with hopelessness or weakness.

Winners, Losers, and Survivors

One of the sad things about divorce is that there really aren't any winners. For all the strategizing and game playing, no one seems to end up the victor. Both parties end up being losers. That is way beyond a bummer. I just wanted to get out and get on and get over it. I didn't want to keep throwing the ball into my husband's court or even receive the ball back in mine. I wanted peace between us, for us to just get along, just share, and just be nice.

My attorney kept me on track, though. I was anxious about surviving the next fifteen to twenty minutes; she was concerned about the next fifteen to twenty years. She wouldn't let me acquiesce or give up. She was like Moses' brother, Aaron, holding up my arms so the battle could be won:

> Whenever Moses held up his hand, Israel prevailed, and whenever he lowered his hand, Amalek prevailed. But Moses' hands grew weary, so they took a stone and put it under him, and he sat on it, while Aaron and Hur held up his hands, one on one side, and the other on the other side. So his hands were steady until the going down of the sun. And Joshua overwhelmed Amalek and his people with the sword. (Exodus 17:11–13, ESV)

Those verses reminded me that the battle was the Lord's, and my job was to stand still, focus on Christ, and wait for His deliverance. And by standing still, I don't mean that I just stood there and let things happen around me. I mean that I quieted my mind and my heart as I trusted that God was working in the midst of my situation, whether I saw it or not. And God was indeed working. Believe me, I understand that there are moments when you may doubt God's involvement and question whether He's really there for you. Cling to your faith in those moments. Faith is trusting what we can't see (Hebrews 11:1). You might need some fresh perspective to see how God is sustaining you through these difficult moments.

When I felt alone, I was reminded that God provided me with friends who loved me and were willing to come alongside me. A few weeks after my husband left, I unexpectedly misplaced my wedding ring. I believe it fell off my finger as a result of my adultery-diet weight loss. I was distraught over losing my ring. It seemed to me to be some sort of horrible sign that all was lost. I know that wasn't the case, but I couldn't understand why God would let that happen on top of everything else. It just seemed cruel.

I wanted to keep that ring on my finger for me and my children and as a testimony to my hope in God. Surprisingly, one of my dearest friends had a wedding band I could wear. Her husband had given her a new one on their anniversary, so she offered me her old one. How blessed I was to wear a ring on my finger that symbolized not only my "for-better-or-worse" covenant but also the love of a precious friend. I wore that ring for many months and didn't remove it until I stepped out of the courtroom after my divorce was finalized.

Every time a friend did something for me that I could check off my to-do list, I felt such relief. It could have been something as simple as cooking dinner for my family or offering to take my youngest children for an hour or two. But for me, the biggest blessing was knowing that people were praying for me. It was a huge relief to know I wasn't alone in my battle for my marriage and family. There were many times when the battle seemed lost, when the victory, as it were, didn't seem worth the effort, when the wounds were unbearably painful. But I knew God had called me to persevere (Ephesians 6:18).

Rejoice in the Lord always; again I will say, Rejoice. Let your reasonableness be known to everyone. The Lord is at hand; do not be anxious about anything, but in everything by prayer and supplication with thanksgiving let your requests be made known to God. And the peace of God, which surpasses all understanding, will guard your hearts and your minds in Christ Jesus.

—PHILIPPIANS 4:4-7, ESV

As you may already know, the divorce process requires a long-range perspective, an understanding that separation and divorce are part of the journey, not the final destination. There is life after divorce, but to a degree, the quality of your life afterward will be determined by your ability to stay strong throughout the process. It's easy to get caught up in and overwhelmed by the day-to-day stuff, but you *have* to think about your future and the future of your children. Be a fighter. Be proactive. Be a step ahead.

That gentle and quiet spirit we want to exhibit is going to have to be a strong and steadfast "gentle and quiet spirit" (1 Peter 3:4). I don't think we ever have to get nasty or vicious in this process. I believe that if we're praying, reading the Bible, and seeking godly counsel, we can absolutely walk through divorce with our heads held high and even come through it with a great testimony. Although there are no real winners, we can be survivors. You and I can be strong and positive survivors whose lives are a testimony to God's faithfulness, provision, and sustaining grace.

Oh, Father, it's so difficult to have to battle with the person we thought would always be our companion, friend, and love. It's so difficult to think about so many practical things when all we want to do is survive this time. Lord, give us strength to stand strong in Your Word (Psalm 119:28). Let us be an example of grace and mercy even as we seek to protect and provide for ourselves and our children.

Father, give us wisdom and insight to know what to pursue and what to let go of. May all we do, even in this mess of a situation, bring You glory. Lord, thank You that You are working in all of this, that You aren't surprised by anything. Lord, thank You that You are more than able to take care of our children and us. Thank You that our security isn't in money or material things but is found solely in You. Your Word says that if we hold fast to You in love, You will deliver, protect, and rescue us. You will be with us in our trouble and answer us when we call (Psalm 91:14–16, ESV). Lord, may our hearts always trust You, our mouths always praise You, and our minds always seek You.

In Jesus' name, amen.

FOUR

Bawling at Bedtime

All your children shall be taught by the LORD, and great shall be the peace of your children.

—ISAIAH 54:13, ESV

So many times I'm struck by an awful pain in my chest when I look at my precious children. I feel an overwhelming sadness that my story of abandonment and pain is their story, too. I would have done anything to keep this from becoming their reality. I wish I could take it all, and they could live blissfully unaware of the grief of abandonment and divorce. But God allowed this ordeal to be part of my story . . . and the story of my children.

For those of us who have gone through divorce, one of the most difficult aspects of this process is that we must graciously walk our children through it as well. If it was just our lives, our circumstances, our pain, we might be able to look at everything differently. It might be a little easier to trust God. I know that makes no sense, really. If I can trust God with my life, why not my children's lives as well? For some reason, when my sweet children are added to the mix—their lives, their circumstances, their pain—I want to take on the world. I want to fix it all so badly. The reality is that I can't; only God can.

During my first meeting with my pastors, I semi-jokingly asked if it would be okay to pray that my husband would have a heart attack before anyone, particularly my children, found out what he had done. After a pause, one pastor replied that he thought it would be okay as I long as I prayed it in God's will. You know, "Lord, if it is Your will, could my husband kick the bucket before this becomes common knowledge?" He was kidding, I think. It was the only time I laughed that week.

I wish I could have done something—anything—to protect my children from this disaster. But I've come to accept that regardless of my desire to shield my children from heartbreak, I cannot. I could not. I'm thankful for the assurance that God will use even this experience to mold them into the men and women He has designed them to be. While it doesn't completely remove the ache or sorrow over what my children have lost, I find comfort in that knowledge.

Hiding the Heartbreak

During the first few weeks of our marital crisis, before anyone knew of my husband's betrayal, I was able, for the most part, to keep what was happening from my children. I'm sure they had an inkling something was going on, because I looked terrible from secretly weeping, and my husband and I were frequently having hushed, serious conversations.

The day after he signed the separation agreement and left the marriage, he came over to the house after work. It was a Friday. We sat the children down on the sofas, and he shared in the most unemotional, detached way that he was moving out. He said he had found someone else and no longer loved me. My fifteen-year-old son placed his head in the crook of his elbow, which was resting on the arm of the sofa. His disappointment and sadness were evident. My twelve-year-old daughter and eight-year-old son both burst into tears—actually, *wailing* would be a more appropriate word. One of my children cried out, "Daddy, no! Please don't go!" Another started wailing something about us being poor and having nowhere to live.

Our children begged and pleaded, but my husband didn't even reach out to comfort them. He didn't touch them. I rushed over and gathered them all in my arms. We held each other and cried. But he didn't engage. In fact, he headed upstairs to grab some of his stuff so that he could begin the process of moving out. I wanted to think that he was acting aloof because he would have lost his resolve to leave if he had allowed himself to feel anything.

The children went to their rooms in tears. As my husband loaded things into his car, my oldest daughter frantically began writing a letter asking him to stay. My youngest son got his father's Bible and followed him around, trying to give it to him. My oldest son just sat in his room. The little girls, nearly three years old and eighteen months, were both playing in their room, unaware, at least on the surface, of the tragedy unfolding around them. I was going from child to child—talking, explaining, praying, crying, and holding.

I don't think there are words to express the magnitude of the misery that played out that afternoon. My children were forever changed. One man's selfish actions destroyed their lives as they knew them. As I followed my husband down the hallway, at one point I realized that I had never understood hate until that moment. I don't think I hated him as much as I hated what he was doing. I might be wrong. I might truly have just hated him.

Years later, I still cannot fathom the destruction that was wrought that day. I can't think about it without a heavy heart. I'd always tried to shield my children from adult issues and emotions, but now they were thrown into a world full of them. Oh that I could have protected my children in some way from this tragedy! But the plain truth is that I couldn't control my husband's actions. I couldn't stop him from leaving. What I could do was help my children navigate this new reality. It became my sole responsibility to protect my family.

The strong woman I wanted to be for my children was often careworn, exhausted, and a tad too emotional for anyone's good. Thankfully, God was faithful to use me even when I was wrestling with trusting Him and believing in myself. He was gracious, compassionate, "slow to anger," and "abounding in love" (Psalm 86:15). And because of His grace, I saw glimpses of those qualities in myself. Many times I felt inadequate for the task of single motherhood, but how I felt wasn't always accurate. The truth was that because I had the Lord in my life, I was indeed able to do it. You may be feeling unable to handle all that is before you, but God can absolutely use you even when you feel inadequate.

God enabled me to provide for my children; function well in an overwhelmed, weary state; and over time, experience the fun and enjoyment of raising my children once again. It was challenging beyond description to walk my children through this crisis, but it was also a time filled with blessings beyond measure. If you are going through this experience right now, I promise you that God can extend blessings even amid the chaos.

Five Children, Five Responses, Five Hundred Conversations, Five Thousand Prayers

Meeting the needs of each of my children proved to be one of the most challenging aspects of my divorce. As expected, each child dealt with their father's departure differently. It was so difficult to discern the best way to encourage them when I desperately needed to be encouraged and healed as well. But in some ways it was helpful to have five other people to consider, because it became impossible to wallow in my own sorrow. I had to get up and move forward—I had five people depending on me.

My oldest son, Zachary, was a young teenager when he suddenly became the man of the house. Within minutes of my husband leaving after his fateful announcement, we were preparing to leave for my parents' home. Zach immediately assumed the responsibility of making sure the house was set up for our absence. I was very proud of him and yet saddened that he had so quickly assumed the man-of-the-house role. It became my goal to keep him from becoming too much of an adult at the age of fifteen.

He was the quintessential firstborn child—hard-working, responsible, and dependable. It appeared that he didn't want to allow himself to feel anything openly. His coping mechanism seemed to be humor, a gift of his we all enjoy immensely. That became another difficulty for me as I tried not to jump into the witty banter, which often had his father as its subject.

If I tried to have serious conversations with Zach, I most often heard, "I'm okay, Mom, really." He wasn't annoyed by my queries; he just wasn't interested in talking about his father or our family situation. I tried not to push it, but I could tell from his humor that he was angry and hurt. Like all my children, I took Zach to counseling. The counselor felt he was handling it well and suggested I just bring him on an as-needed basis. I think my son considered "as needed" to be never.

During this period, I sought a counselor's advice about different situations with Zach. For example, although he was always respectful in his father's presence, at home he started calling his father by his first name. This seemed disrespectful to me. The counselor I spoke to suggested that I allow Zach to speak openly with me about his father. This meant that if Zach wanted to call his father by his first name at home, it was fine. If he wanted to make comments about his father, as long as they weren't completely over the line, I should let them go. If he wanted to joke around and deal with everything with humor, that was okay too.

I had been so worried that I should be correcting it all, telling my kids to respect their dad, period. And honestly, I was proud of my children, because they were always respectful and kind to their father in his presence, as far as I knew. It was just at home that the sarcasm flowed. All my children were quick with humor, but they weren't always kind when it came to joking about their dad.

Other than his droll dialogue, Zach didn't share much about his thoughts regarding his father. He still doesn't. I have watched his progress, though. He initially seemed very angry, which came out in his humor, in the way he acted while playing sports, and in his impatience with his siblings. But that calmed considerably after the first year of the divorce.

When his anger was at its worst, I was told that it was important to get him into sports so he could work out the emotions he was feeling through physical activities. That was undeniably very effective. As his anger subsided, his sarcasm did too. It was replaced by much more positive humor. He seemed to begin to accept the situation for what it was and learn to work through it without anger or bitterness.

I still see, in little actions and comments, his disappointment in his father, but he has remained a respectful and kind young man. I believe that allowing him to express his emotions in the way that was best for him has enabled him to reach a place of healing and strength. His faith is stronger than ever, and I am very proud of the fine young man he has become.

My oldest daughter, Emma, was a preteen when her father left. Some would say she was at the most important age for a father to be involved and attentive to her. I would agree, except that it felt as if each of my children was at an important age for their father to be there. She was extremely upset the day he left but quickly became almost unemotional about it. Like her older brother, she didn't want to discuss it much at all. Our conversations were short.

I could tell she desperately wanted her daddy's love and attention even after he left. By abandoning all of us, he had failed miserably to provide her with that security. The difficulty for my twelve-year-old daughter was that no man could really step in and be a daddy figure for her. No man could love on her like her daddy was designed to. No man we knew could pull her onto his lap and hold her tight. My heart ached for her loss.

I did take her to counseling as well. Again the counselor felt she didn't need counseling regularly. At the time that seemed all right to me. I felt it was better to deal with the situation as a family. I would say that in hindsight, I think more counseling might have been beneficial. Not because I saw any problems but because it would have been a blessing to talk to someone who wasn't emotionally involved.

My children had friends to talk to, but that definitely wasn't the same as an adult who was trained to walk someone through the challenges associated with divorce. Thankfully, Emma and I have a very open and honest relationship in which she knows she has the freedom and safety to share or not share, and I will love her nonetheless.

About two years after her father left, I took Emma on a FamilyLife Passport2Purity weekend. We had a lovely time and were able to talk about a lot of things, although we didn't discuss anything involving her father and his mistress. On the way home, I asked if she wanted to talk about anything regarding the situation we found ourselves in as a family.

She replied, "No, that's okay. I'm just gonna wait until I'm older and have a bunch of relationship issues." We both laughed, but I prayed fervently that this wouldn't be the case. Unfortunately, I know a lot of data suggests that young girls her age whose fathers leave the home might have some serious relationship issues later on. But my children are not statistics, and I refuse to allow them to become such. Instead, I am covering them in prayer, pouring it over them like syrup on pancakes.

The wonderful relationship Emma and I have developed despite all we've been through has been an unexpected blessing for me. Dealing with adolescence alone with her was an intimidating thought. I feared not having the buffer of a father between us, but God proved He was more than able to handle the role of buffer.

My daughter and I have grown closer as we've walked this path together. Getting ready together in the morning has become our daily routine, and late-night conversations have become the norm. She comfortably shares stories of her day with me and even supports me leading a Bible study for her and her friends at our home. She seems proud of our relationship. Recently she shared how thankful she is that we have such a great relationship. I feel incredibly grateful too.

My youngest son, Peter, my middle child, was the most open with his thoughts concerning his father's decision to leave us. He asked the most questions; had the longest, most frequent conversations with me; and showed the most emotion. I struggled as I tried to help him, because it was gut-wrenching to deal with his inquiries and comments. He had so many difficult questions from the moment his father left. He was trying to make something that was impossible to understand understandable.

He and I prayed a lot together. He felt his father's betrayal keenly and sought to rescue me from the effects of it. To be honest, I was unsure how to help him. Out of all of my children, Peter has received the most counseling. He would even occasionally request it. He responded positively to having someone with whom to share his thoughts, struggles, and questions. The counselor understood his need to talk and was a good sounding board. I didn't always know what they discussed, but my son always emerged from the room in a good mood. He seemed to need the chance to say aloud, "This stuff stinks!"

I realized that Peter needed time—time to process, time to heal, and time with me. I tried being compassionate to the point of coddling him at first, but that seemed to encourage more emotion. Then I tried being firm and almost drill sergeantish with him, but that made us both unhappy and seemed punitive where punishment wasn't warranted. Success came when I realized he just needed me to be Mom and stop trying to figure out how to fix him. I decided to love on him as any mother would love on her son and focus on raising him to be a godly young man. I answered his questions when I could and in an age-appropriate way.

My older children were often annoyed by his questions, comments, and discussions about their dad. They believed that it hurt me to talk about it. Maybe it hurt them to think about it. I explained that we all process things differently. I wanted us to allow each other to deal with our hurt in whatever way we needed to, within reason. There were a lot of people grieving in our home, whether it was done openly or not. We were like big bruises painfully bumping into each other. I wanted us to be gentle and loving with one another. It wasn't always easy—even for me, the supposed adult of the family.

One of the most surprising things I encountered with Peter was his quest for information. He wanted to know everything, and when I say *everything*, I really mean everything. He was angry at me for quite a while because I didn't tell him immediately when I found out about his father's affair. He felt it was his right to know. He was frustrated that I wasn't willing to share details of his father's actions. He was annoyed that I didn't keep him in the loop when we were working through the issues of separation and divorce.

It was the weirdest thing to have my eight-year-old request information about things no eight-year-old should be privy to or even know about. I had to stand firm in the face of his demands. There was no way I was going to give him details or keep him abreast of the situation. Too much information would only have confused him and caused him more pain. I also believe it would have been a never-ending search for more and more knowledge that was simply too complicated, emotional, and difficult for him to process.

Instead, I shared with him a story about Corrie ten Boom and her father, which she had included in her book *The Hiding Place*. Corrie had asked her father a difficult question regarding an adult issue. She wrote,

"He turned to look at me, as he always did when answering a question, but to my surprise he said nothing. At last he stood up, lifted his traveling case from the rack over our heads, and set it on the floor. 'Will you carry it off the train, Corrie?' he said."

Corrie stood up and tried unsuccessfully to lift the case.

"It's too heavy," she told her father.

"Yes," he replied. "And it would be a pretty poor father who would ask his little girl to carry such a load. It's the same way, Corrie, with knowledge. Some knowledge is too heavy for children. When you are older and stronger you can bear it. For now you must trust me to carry it for you."*

I think Peter understood the point I was trying to make, but it only stopped his questions for a moment. I wasn't sure why he had such a quest for knowledge, except that maybe he thought he could figure it all out and fix it if he just had more information. I wish I could have done that myself.

Although he received the most counseling and seemed to work through his emotions more openly than my other children, I was often most concerned about him. Peter seemed to be the most negatively affected by the divorce, and I was frequently uncertain how to deal with it. I wanted to raise him to be a strong and stable young man who didn't feel the need to dwell on the negative or manipulate the situation to his advantage. What I found was that honesty truly was the best policy with him. We talked things through appropriately and candidly. We prayed about everything. And we asked forgiveness of each other often. This approach provided him with a safe place to work through things and has enabled him to heal and find peace.

My two youngest daughters, Elizabeth and Allison, were so little when their daddy left that it wasn't an issue for quite a while. These two

---

* Corrie ten Boom, with John and Elizabeth Sherrill, *The Hiding Place* (New York: Bantam Books, 1971), 26–27.

precious little girls are my special gifts, adopted through foster care. When I think about the way the first several years of their lives have gone, I want to weep buckets. It hurts me deeply to know that three out of four of their parents have acted very selfishly. They are wonderful and deserve parents who love them selflessly. It terrifies me that I will fail them in some way too.

They are both very sweet, but oh so spicy as well. God is going to do great things with these strong-willed little people, of that I'm confident. It's just a challenge teaching them to use their powers for good!

More than a year after my husband left, they began to recognize that things weren't as they should be. Their questions were heartbreaking and extremely difficult to answer. Each answer I gave seemed to lead to more unanswerable questions. They didn't understand much of what had happened. They would ask where their daddy was and why he didn't live with us anymore. That would lead to more questions about what had happened and why. Did I love him? Did he love me? Why was he with a different lady?

I couldn't always figure out how to answer their questions in age-appropriate ways. I often just said, "I don't know, sweetie," and "I loved your daddy very much," and "Daddy loved me very much when we got married," and "You can talk to Daddy about that, sweetheart."

My answers never seemed enough to them or to me. They seemed to accept my attempts at answers, but I could see the confusion in their eyes. There were no easy answers to big questions posed by my little people. Eventually we just got to the place where they accepted, for the most part, the situation for what it was, and we adjusted as a family.

The tricky thing with my little girls was that they knew how to work any situation to their advantage. Maybe you've experienced this with your children. My youngest, Allison, would often call for her daddy in the saddest, most pitiful wail when she was in trouble. Elizabeth would talk about how Daddy wouldn't do that, wouldn't say that, would allow that, wouldn't discipline her, or a thousand other things that simply drove me bonkers. There were times when I wanted to respond, "Well, you know what? Daddy isn't here, is he?" Thankfully I kept my mouth shut, because I would have been talking out of hurt rather than being the mommy I wanted to be.

I learned to not say a whole lot when those issues came up. I would attempt to comfort when comfort was required, and I would continue with consequences when necessary. They eventually gave up on this ploy, because the reality was that their daddy wasn't going to jump in and save them from the discipline they deserved. He wouldn't have done that even if he had been at home. That lesson was one all my children had to learn; it was just a little more heartbreaking because of the circumstances.

Again, I was learning that my parenting hadn't changed much. In fact, it was important that it didn't change. My children needed the stability of knowing that although our circumstances had changed, I was still going to be the same ole mom and treat them like the same ole kids.

Friends often remind me that God entrusted each of my children to me because I was made to be their mommy. He has uniquely equipped me to parent them, even as a single parent. I believe that most of us struggle with something related to our parenting. For me, I just wish I was better about structure, organization, and unemotional parenting. Not three of my gifts, to be sure. We all want to do this parenting thing perfectly, which, unfortunately, is impossible.

Again, what God is showing me is that it isn't about my doing something perfectly, better, or even differently, or about changing my circumstances or environment; it's simply about being who I am in Christ. I know I won't parent flawlessly, but I will do it tenderly and with as much joy as I possibly can.

My Children and Their Father

I've shared a lot about my relationship with my children, but their relationship with their father is equally important, although a little more challenging. My children, regardless of what their father has done, will always love him. He will always be their father. My job is to make sure they have the best relationship they can have with him. A big part of their happiness and comfort in that relationship is dependent on my attitude.

At times I can sense that they're watching me to detect what I think about something involving their father. I have to be sure to encourage them to have as healthy a relationship with him as possible. That means I positively support visits with their dad. It also means I don't make comments that might cause my children to feel guilty or conflicted about their time with or feelings for their dad. Holding my tongue, controlling my facial expressions, and generally curbing my negative thoughts are good habits I'm trying to develop so that my attitude will bless my children. I'm not saying it's easy, but it's necessary.

At first it was especially difficult to encourage my children to spend time with their dad. He was essentially a stranger to all of us, and my children didn't want to spend time with him. The first several months after he left, he didn't pursue time with them. When he finally saw them, their visits were awkward and uncomfortable for everyone, and I was faced with having to be their social coordinator. Definitely not the easiest job I've undertaken. I suggested outings, encouraged one-on-one visits, tried to say yes whenever he requested any time with any of the children, and basically just tried to have a cheerful outlook whenever possible. It took time, a concerted effort, and a fair amount of prayer, but it got easier as we all adapted to the new situation.

Part of my children's discomfort was their concern that wanting to spend time with their father would hurt me. I had to encourage them that it didn't. It was okay that they still loved him. It was okay that they sometimes wanted to be with him. Even if, to be truthful, it didn't feel completely okay, I had to get past my own hurt so that I could do what was best for my children. I knew how important it was for them to have a relationship with their father.

My children continue to need to know that I support their decisions and emotions regarding their father. In all honesty, I haven't been 100 percent successful at this. I want to be the super-supportive mom of my dreams, but there are definitely times when I slip up and make a snarky comment about how late their father is or how he canceled a visit or didn't show up for soccer games. It's impossible to be perfect in this area. But for my children's sake, it's important that I at least strive for perfection. So I keep trying. I'm sure you can relate.

My heart's desire is that my children's relationships with the Lord will sustain them through all the questions, pain, and choices that lie ahead. We are honest in our discussions about their father's adultery and abandonment, but I endeavor to keep my words positive, respectful, and affirming rather than negative and discouraging. They also know that their father still loves them and that it's more than okay that they love him, too.

My children and their father are doing much better now. He still isn't the father he once was, but I see him making more efforts. He invites them to do more things with him as individuals and as a group. He and I have been able to have pleasant conversations about different issues involving each of our children. And I'm finally at a place where I'm actually happy for them all. I'm so glad that he isn't a stranger to them anymore. And I'm especially thankful that we're all functioning quite well in our new family situation. It's not ideal, but we're making it work.

My Children and Our Families

Another profound impact of divorce is the sudden loss of relationships with in-laws and ex-spouses' extended families. It shouldn't be surprising, but it can often come as a shock when people we've known and loved for years suddenly no longer want anything to do with us. The result is very often a new wave of rejection and loneliness.

We need a new grace to deal with in-laws and the changed dynamics of these relationships. Unfortunately, we typically experience the loss of our marriages and our relationships with our in-laws simultaneously. Maybe some of you are saying, "That wasn't actually a bad thing!" Point taken. I know many divorcees who would agree that the loss of a relationship with their in-laws wasn't a particularly difficult thing to accept. But our children need to know that no matter the difficulties of our relationships with their grandparents, they are still encouraged to love them, talk to them, and visit them.

For some of us, the transition will be awkward but not awful. I'm blessed to have a father-in-law who is a Christian. We have worked through some of the difficulties and have quite a good relationship. From the very beginning, I told him that I wouldn't do anything to jeopardize his relationship with his grandchildren. I knew that no matter what happened between his son and me, he would want a healthy, loving relationship with his grandchildren.

We don't talk often, but when my father-in-law and his wife visit our area, they spend a good amount of time with my children and me. I have asked if my ex-husband would like more time with my in-laws whenever they're in town, but he has declined each time. I think maybe someday that will change, but right now I'm thankful that my children can rest in the knowledge that we adults have put aside all the mess and are just here to love on them.

I know this isn't always the case. I have one friend who lost all her relationships with her in-laws and extended family when her husband left her and her children. It's baffling and yet understandable at the same time. It's baffling because I know this woman to be extraordinary, loving, and just the bee's knees. Her husband, on the other hand, has most definitely not been anything resembling the knees on a bee. And yet her in-laws' decision to side with her ex-husband and distance themselves from her is understandable at the same time, because . . . well, what's a parent to do?

We can pray that our parents or in-laws would always act maturely and face the facts of a situation, but unfortunately that isn't always the case. Sometimes it's easier for parents to turn a blind eye to their loved one's failings rather than face them head-on and deal with the consequences. Sometimes it's just too difficult for in-laws to deal with the abandoned spouse because it might mean taking sides against their own flesh and blood, and they'd really like to avoid that.

It's painful to deal with the sister-in-law who used to be a dear friend and yet now refuses to talk to you. It's heartbreaking to know that a mother-in-law will avoid calling her grandchildren so she doesn't have to talk to her former daughter-in-law. It's infuriating to be painted as the bad guy in a situation where you're most definitely not the one wearing the black hat. But despite the injustice, it's important to work through the difficulties with a gracious attitude.

My friend struggles with how to have a positive attitude toward her in-laws. She's been treated very unfairly and unkindly, but she has children who still need to have a relationship with their grandparents. She tried to defend her side of the story while knowing it would be impossible to change their minds. Quite expectedly, she didn't receive any positive feedback.

She shared with me that maybe her motivation wasn't as much to make things better between them as it was to justify herself. Ultimately, she recognized that defending herself wasn't where her focus needed to be. It needed to be on navigating her children and herself through these new circumstances with kindness, dignity, and strength. She found the strength to offer grace because she took the focus off herself, her need for validation, and even her desire to be treated fairly. It was about becoming the best woman and mother she could be by praying, renewing her mind in God's Word, and having others help her stay accountable of her actions.

She shared that working and being productive—whether as a mom, a homemaker, an office assistant, or a counselor—also helped her deal with all the variables of divorce, including lost relationships. She has found this seemingly simple focus invaluable in keeping her from sliding into anger and bitterness.

The best thing you can do when faced with losing relationships with your ex-spouse's family is to keep communication open on your end as best you can. I suspect that a very good first step would be to write a simple letter or e-mail stating very clearly and succinctly that it is not your desire to sever all ties between your children and their grandparents or other family members. Maybe setting up a nonconfrontational way to plan those visits or phone calls could also be done through e-mail. If your children are older, allow or even encourage them to make phone calls, send e-mails, or write letters to their grandparents. Try to remember birthdays, anniversaries, and holidays with cards. I know that it isn't "fun" to do these things, but it will bless your children, and that's what is most important.

When you do have the opportunity to communicate with your ex-spouse's family, keeping your conversations free of negative comments about your ex-spouse and avoiding revealing any information that would imply you want family members to take sides is imperative. In other words, share positive information only. That old adage "If you can't say something nice, don't say anything at all" is absolutely applicable. I know it's challenging, because sometimes there's just so much tempting material at your disposal, but fight the urge to speak unkind and disparaging words.

My Children and Me

My poor kids get a massive dose of Mom all the time. Sometimes that's a great thing; sometimes not so much. I've made more mistakes, said more dumb things, vented more emotions (good and bad) than I should have, shared more than I ought, and expressed my opinion more often than necessary. I've been petty about things when I should have been more mature.

I've made a lot of mistakes, but despite them all, my children are doing very well, especially considering the stuff we've been through. My family is pretty normal, too. Apart from stressing about things too often, I think I'm beginning to figure out this single-mom thing.

I know that I can't change my family's circumstances to the degree I want to, nor can I change my children's emotions, responses, or behavior. But I can endeavor to respond with grace, patience, and love and to be the best mom I can be for my family.

I pray fervently for my children, and I encourage you to do the same for your children. My children have seen the consequences of their father's choices and understand intimately the pain these choices have caused. That knowledge, I believe, will enable them to be strong if they ever face similar temptations. I'm confident that God is going to use this experience to make my children stronger, wiser, and more compassionate people. It is my prayer that I will be instrumental in that process in their lives. I pray that God will use me mightily to bless my children.

Lord, our hearts break for our children and all the other children who are suffering through divorce, abandonment, and the aftereffects of adultery. Oh, God, we know that it is never Your will that a marriage end, certainly not like this, but we do know that You can work it all for good if we will love You and trust You (Romans 8:28).

Father, give us the discernment we need to encourage our children and the insight to know what will bless them most (Philippians 1:9–11). Hold our tongues when we want to say what we really think but shouldn't (Psalm 141:3). Let us speak only words of life—words that edify and encourage (Psalm 19:14).

Give us strength, Lord, for the tasks we face as single parents (2 Thessalonians 2:16–17). Grant us wisdom and knowledge to lead our families well. Help us to be consistent and diligent in our prayer lives, our parenting, our discipline, and our own walk with You. Father, when all we're dealing with seems too much to bear, please strengthen us through Your Word and hide us in Your shelter (Psalm 27:5). God, please be our "refuge and strength," an "ever-present help in times of trouble" (Psalm 46:1). Help us model faith and perseverance for our children. May our homes be filled with the fruit of Your Spirit: love, joy, peace, patience, kindness, goodness, faithfulness, gentleness, and self-control (Galatians 5:22).

May our children be strengthened in their faith, bold in their Christian walk, and passionate in their love for You. God, please be glorified and honored in our families.

In Jesus' name, amen.

FIVE

Forgiveness: Trading the Unbearable for the Beautiful

Let the peace of Christ rule in your hearts.

—COLOSSIANS 3:15

Above all, love each other deeply, because love covers over a multitude of sins.

—1 PETER 4:8

Forgiveness. It's something we'd like to always be the recipient of, but not necessarily something we always want to offer. We have a natural tendency to look at someone else's behavior and compare it to our own— usually to our advantage. I, for one, am quite adept at elevating myself in my own mind when it comes to my ability to handle life's difficulties, to rise above a situation, or to judge my own sin as so much "lighter" than someone else's. As if God has different levels of sin based on caloric or fat intake—sin-free, sin-lite, sinless, 2 percent sin, 80/15 sin content.

It's easy in our worldly wisdom to think that certain sins are so much worse than others, and according to our laws, it's true. And yet in God's court of law, there are only two simple categories: sinful and sinless. Please don't think I'm implying that something like fussing at someone is on the same level as committing adultery. What I *am* saying is that we all struggle with sin, and because of that, we're all guilty of sinning. We "*all* have sinned and fall short of the glory of God" (Romans 3:23, emphasis added).

I once heard our efforts to conquer sin as a race to get across the ocean. We're on one shore of the ocean, and God is on another. If each

Journal entry: Today I offered my husband forgiveness. I wanted to talk to him in person, but since he is married and I'm a single woman, that seemed problematic. How strange that the man I was married to for so long can no longer be alone with me. I ended up writing him a letter. I told him that I had forgiven him and that I did hope for good things for him. I told him that there might still be times when I get upset about the consequences of his actions on our children, but that I would try to continually forgive.

I can't remember everything I said, but I tried to be kind and positive in my approach. I wasn't sure if he would respond, but later that night he texted, "Thank you." I was shocked and so very thankful—and so very, very sad. I wish things were different, but this is where we are, and I need to move forward and quit looking back. That's part of forgiveness, after all, right?

I'm incredibly thankful that I finally got to the point of being able to forgive. It feels so freeing, and I think it's going to be great for my kids. Lord, thank You for bringing me to this point. I pray that he will one day actually seek forgiveness from You and me and our children. I pray that forgiveness will lead the way to restoring his relationship with You. Amen.

of us could swim only as far as our righteousness allowed, we would all still be woefully short of His shoreline. Some of us might make it past the breakers, and others might make it out into the open seas, but really, we would all be in need of rescuing shortly after our adventure began. The idea of any of us making it to the other side of the ocean based on our own ability and merit is impossible.

After we've been so grievously wounded by our ex-spouses, who covenanted with us to be faithful in life and love, it's often a struggle to fully grasp our own need for forgiveness. I mean, we all know we're sinners—it's a given. I yell at my kids way too much. I can't seem to get my thoughts to remain on all that is true, noble, right, pure, lovely, admirable, excellent, and praiseworthy (Philippians 4:8). I selfishly want things my way. I'm basically your overworked, overwhelmed, overwrought, overcommitted single mom who is hanging by a slowly unraveling thread. But when I compare myself to my ex-husband, I look pretty good. At least I didn't do *that*! But while I've never committed adultery, I cannot deny that I've done other things I'm not particularly proud of. That's reality.

We all struggle with things we wish we didn't. But in pointing this out, I'm not trying to heap guilt on anyone. Goodness knows, we all have moments of anger and frustration that result in us yelling at our children. And there isn't a person in this world who doesn't wrestle with thoughts that are less than noble. We're all in need of forgiveness. We all make mistakes.

I think maybe it's more about what we do with our mistakes and sins. We need to seek God's forgiveness and remember that He still loves us despite our failures. As we receive God's forgiveness, we'll find hope and healing for the things we've done as well as the things that have been done to us. In many ways, it's blessedly easy to receive forgiveness, but it's exceedingly difficult to offer it. And yet that is just what we need to do, my friend.

FALLING SHORT

I felt closer to God the year my husband left than I ever have. I felt completely upheld by His mercy, cared for by His grace, and sustained by His love. The second year was much more difficult, not because God changed, but because I did. I found myself no longer leaning heavily on Him but rather trying to figure things out on my own. I was living in doubt rather than trusting in God's faithfulness. I was trying to take things into my own hands, trying to make things happen the way I wanted them to happen. Honestly, it didn't work out very well for me.

I found that the more I took things into my own hands, the more I struggled with *everything*. I realized that my issue, at the core, was not trusting God. I knew in my heart and mind that He was completely trustworthy, but I wasn't acting like it. I kept trying to be in charge, and in the process, I ran roughshod over my relationship with God. I even went so far as not heeding His obvious leading, the paths out of temptation He made available, and His provision for my life.

The challenges, struggles, and temptations I faced daily were so overwhelming that at times I wanted to curl up in a ball and hide. I knew that most often my struggles were because I had chosen my own way rather than God's. I was easily swayed by the world's way of looking at things—how my life should look, how I should feel, what my level of happiness should be, and how everyone should act. I measured my success not by Scripture but by the way I thought things should be. It was surprisingly easy to turn my thoughts to the things of this world.

It was equally easy to overlook the right thing to do or think just so I could feel comfort, pleasure, and ease. I was so embarrassed by my own tendencies that I found it difficult to share my struggles with anyone. It made me want to avoid my friends, who I knew would discern my inner conflict. Lest you spend the rest of the book wondering, let me share one of those tendencies. I very much wanted to fix my situation, and at the time, I believed the best way to do so was with a man. I wanted any man. I didn't expect much, except for wanting someone I could get along with and who loved me. Although looking back, I think even if he had really just liked me a lot, I would have been okay with it.

I was willing to do anything to secure a new relationship. I had conversations in my head that went something like this: *I did it right for forty years, and look where it got me! Maybe I'll just do it the other way and see how it works out! Or, I tried to be a good wife. I was faithful to my husband. I didn't abandon my marriage, so why shouldn't I have some of the perks of marriage now? So what if I'm not married or even in love. Who would know? What would it matter?*

Thankfully I didn't follow through on my thinking. But I desperately struggled because the opportunities were there. I unquestionably was tempted. As I tried to maintain my godly woman exterior and deal with my very rebellious interior, my inner turmoil began to affect every area of my life.

When my carefully crafted facade started to crumble, and my struggle began to show through, I knew something needed to change—and that something was me. I prayed that God would take away the things that were tempting me and help me with all my struggles. He answered my prayer, but I also had to make the difficult choices to fight those temptations.

I had to stop putting myself in situations I knew would only cause me to go backward in my battle. For me, that meant ending some relationships with friends who encouraged me to pursue that way of thinking. I also had to tell trusted friends what I was dealing with. I had to be honest. I worked hard to get myself back on solid ground mentally, emotionally, and spiritually.

In the midst of my weakness, God continued to be faithful, continued to pursue me, and continued to love me through my friends and family. One day when I felt particularly defeated by my reaction to my circumstances, a friend reminded me, out of the blue, that God loved me unconditionally. I needed that reminder. When friends or acquaintances shared how my life had inspired them, I wanted to weep because I knew the true nature of my heart, and it was anything but inspiring.

> *One great paradox of the Christian life is that we are fully responsible for our Christian growth and at the same time fully dependent upon the Holy Spirit to give us both the desire to grow and the ability to do it. God's grace does not negate the need for responsible action on our part, but rather makes it possible.*
>
> —Jerry Bridges,
> *Transforming Grace*

I thought often that if people knew me—really knew me—they would be so disappointed. Yet God generously gave me loving friends, scripture that encouraged me, and the resolve to keep going when I felt like giving up. And He still used me to bless my children. He also provided innumerable opportunities for me to encourage others suffering through relationship issues. He opened doors for me to write about my life and experiences.

We have to keep in mind that God doesn't expect perfection from us, nor does He expect us to do something profound for Him. All He wants from us are hearts willing to love and trust Him. If we're willing, He will use us to help others.

FACING THE FACADE

Facing my own temptations and my stubborn impulse to handle things my way instead of God's brought me to a place I might actually have needed to be. It wasn't a pleasant place, but it was a necessary place. As I pondered and dealt with my own sinful nature, my heart began to hurt for my ex-husband. Sin was an easy snare to get caught in (Hebrews 12:1). And he was and is ensnared.

I wondered if he struggled with sin and despaired of ever gaining victory over it. Did he understand God's unconditional love and mercy, which would have enabled him to get back up again? What if he never really understood that we all struggle with sin, but our Savior is big enough to handle it? What if he never felt the peace that comes from falling at our Savior's feet and thanking Him for tossing all our sins "as far as the east is from the west" (Psalm 103:12)? Did my ex-husband understand grace? What if he thought he was the only one struggling and failing? I suspect he might have felt terribly alone in his battle.

Several years before our divorce, my husband purchased the Casting Crowns songbook *Lifesong* because he wanted me to sing "Stained Glass Masquerade" for our church. The lyrics ask, "Is there anyone that fails? Is there anyone that falls? Am I the only one in church today feelin' so small?"

The song describes someone who looks around at church but can't find anyone else who is struggling. Like many of us, he fears that people will find out he doesn't belong, so he decides to bury his struggle and pretend that "everything's okay."*

If I could, I'd include a recording of that song with this book. The words are profound to me. The song asks how the church would greet us if we shared our secrets, showed who we really are. About a year after our divorce was finalized, I heard that song on the radio and remembered that my ex-husband had once asked me to sing it.

I thought about the fact that I might have missed a really great opportunity to bless him. Maybe I'm making something out of nothing, but I don't think so. He had never asked that of me before. Unfortunately, I never took the time to transpose it into the soprano range so I could sing

---

* Mark Hall and Nichole Nordeman, "Stained Glass Masquerade," Lifesong, copyright © 2005, Reunion Records.

it. Regardless, even if my ex-husband just liked the tune, God used the lyrics to soften my heart in preparation for me to forgive.

I wish my ex-husband had understood that grace wasn't something he needed to work for or deserve. I wish he could have shared his inward struggles of desiring other women with someone. I assume it was a struggle for him, because the man I knew would not have blithely plunged into adultery. I can only surmise his thinking and assume the attitude of his heart and mind. I choose to believe that he was a good man who lost a very costly battle.

Pursuing Pardon

Let me say first that at this point, my ex-husband has neither repented nor asked for my forgiveness. I forgave him not because I'm anything special but because I knew that it was the most important step I could take in my own healing.

Forgiveness doesn't mean that we take away the consequences of our offender's actions, nor does it mean we forget. I believe that forgiveness allows me to say that although someone's actions hurt me very much, that person and those actions will not dictate how I feel, live, or think, either now or in the future. Really, so much of the healing process is about our willingness to capture our thoughts and stop the descent into bitterness, revenge, and anger. No healing can take place when we hold on to those caustic emotions. And the only way to release them effectively is to forgive.

Forgiveness for me looked like this: First, I made a conscious decision to forgive my ex-husband; then I asked God to help me forgive. Next, I determined not to entertain angry, bitter, or vengeful thoughts. And then I acted out that forgiveness in my interactions with my ex-husband. Four not-so-easy steps. Each step had its own set of challenges. I decided to forgive because I was convinced that it was the only way I could survive this difficult period in my life with joy and peace in my heart.

I knew that I had to get past the desire to punish and get on with the healing. The initial decision to forgive was probably the easiest step in some ways because it's easy to reach a conclusion and still not truly act on it. Acting on it proved to be the most difficult. I prayed for God's help, but His way of assisting me was a bit different than I thought it would be.

I imagined that God would just shower me with a supernatural ability to look at my ex-husband with love and kindness. Instead, as I have shared, God showed me the state of my own heart. And as I realized that I had some pretty rotten stuff in my heart and mind, God changed my heart toward my ex-husband. I saw him differently. When I saw him as a man lost in his own selfishness, separated from any true peace or hope, and willing to give up all the good in his life for sensual pleasure, I had a measure of compassion—a very small measure, but some nonetheless.

Finally, I had to implement what God had shown me, what I felt convicted to do. I had to treat my ex-husband in a way that didn't make him feel judged or condemned. I had always tried to treat him well, but I knew I had withheld kindness at times during our divorce process and after it was finalized. I had also harbored hopes that he would experience some seriously awful consequences for his actions. I had to no longer envision him getting a terrible illness or living in a box on a street corner. Instead, I had to choose to pray for his healing and reconciliation with God. I had to resolve to be kind in my thinking and my actions. Difficult? Very. But it did get easier over time.

I know that allowing myself to forgive my ex-husband even without him deserving or asking for it has allowed me to have a positive outlook on my life and my children's lives, not tainted by unbridled anger or vengeful thoughts.

Addressing Abandonment

Adultery, abandonment, and divorce are pandemic in our communities and our churches. Obviously, a lot of people are dealing with these issues, and they shouldn't feel alone. I want to reach out to all those people. But I must ask, "Why are so many people dealing with adultery and divorce?" I think a lot has to do with the idea that we can achieve happiness here on earth. That if something is difficult and challenging, we should be free to pursue something that isn't challenging or difficult. Our culture portrays love as a feeling, not a commitment and a choice. That leads to the assumption that when marriage gets difficult or when our spouse isn't all we hoped he or she would be, we have an out.

Why not go find someone else who makes us feel better, at least for this moment in time? We can always move on again if necessary. It is beyond sad. We miss so much when we give up. So many people forfeit the beauty of rising above their circumstances and growing together through adversity for the ease of abandonment and divorce—if either of those can be considered easy.

I also think that if we could only open up and share our struggles, we would find strength to fight the temptation to give it all up. When we name our sins and place them in the light, their power is diminished. The trouble is that there aren't that many safe places where we can openly share our struggles without shame or regret, because people tend to judge so severely.

I think we try to give the impression that we have it all together, and yet most, if not all, of us don't. I guess I should only speak for myself, but I suspect that we all have something we struggle with, something we wish we could purge from our lives. It has struck me deeply that if we were all more honest about our struggles, we could strengthen one another. We would be able to face together what we all try to face alone.

We could walk alongside each other as accountability partners, prayer partners, companions, and friends. Our focus wouldn't be on hiding our issues but rather on conquering them. Our churches would be places that welcomed the broken openly as we all embraced the strength that is offered through Christ.

People would likely accept and applaud our willingness to share some sins openly, but others would be deemed too controversial, too wicked, too . . . well . . . too sinful. I think we put sexual sin in that category all too often. It seems to be the predominant sin in our society, and yet it's the one we least want to deal with openly. It destroys lives, marriages, and families and can continue to do so for generations. It's a reality we should address.

We all struggle with sin. Why is one person's struggle with envy and selfishness any less awful than someone else's struggle with pornography and sexual immorality? At the root, aren't all of them about seeking fulfillment and satisfaction in something other than God? Aren't they both found in sinners in need of a Savior? Didn't Jesus associate with sinners of all shapes, sizes, and sins, and didn't He love them all? He didn't shun them but rather addressed their sin with compassion and grace. Why do we pretend that we can live this life without God, without His strength, without His power, without each other? Why do we think that we must fight our biggest battles alone? What if we allowed others to share their bad stuff with us, and we responded with love and gentleness instead of fear and judgment? What if it was safe for all of us to share our struggles without fear? What if we could truly understand what it means to restore someone gently with humility and love (Galatians 6:1; Ephesians 4:2)? Now that sounds like the way relationships should be!

I discovered what true friendship really looked like when I shared my trials and temptations with my closest friends. They didn't let me get away with anything. They still held me to a godly standard, but they did it with gentleness, compassion, and love. Don't get me wrong, they totally called me on the carpet on a few things. I can laugh about it now, although at the time I was a bit peeved. How thankful I am that I had people in my life who were willing to risk my irritation to speak truthfully into my situation! That experience has made me committed to honesty and truthfulness in my relationships. I avoid conflict like the plague, so that's a big, uncomfortable commitment for me.

As I've shared honestly with trusted friends and family about my struggles, I have found that I'm really not alone. And that has made me more determined than ever to provide a safe place for others to share their struggles. I don't feel called to counseling; I feel called to friendship—honest, beautiful, strengthening friendship. If people around you are going through abandonment or divorce (or any type of struggle), I entreat you to be a safe place for them to talk about their fears and problems.

Dear friend, you have been sinned against greatly, but please don't allow the magnitude of that sin to diminish your own need for a Savior. Don't allow bitterness or self-righteousness to invade your life. It would be a tragedy to survive this ordeal only to find that bitterness has taken root and self-righteousness has overtaken you.

We might look pretty good outwardly as we walk this difficult path, but in reality, we know that we are all walking wounded. Thankfully, our God is bigger than our sorrows and our sins. We can trust Him to handle our situations. We don't have to concern ourselves with figuring out what an appropriate punishment is for our offenders. God will hold those who have sinned against us accountable (Romans 12:19–21; Hebrews 10:30–31). It is our responsibility to accept the grace and strength He offers us in order to forgive and heal.

As Christians, we are children of the King—the merciful, compassionate, faithful King who loves us beyond our comprehension. Let us focus on who we are in Christ rather than trying to compare and contrast ourselves with others. With the Lord's help, we can forgive those who have hurt us, find healing, and see God work in our lives. We are worth far more than we can imagine.

Lord, we come before You as broken people in need of forgiveness, grace, strength, and comfort (Hebrews 4:14–16). It's difficult not to compare ourselves and our seemingly insignificant sins to those who have caused us so much pain. Lord, may our hearts never be hardened to the fact that we need You too. Reveal the sins in our hearts and lives that need to be placed at the foot of the cross and left there. Please forgive us, Lord, if we have chosen to judge others, chosen to look at the speck in someone else's eye and forgotten the plank in our own (Matthew 7:1–5).

God, we can't deny that at times we feel as if our ex-spouses have giant planks in their eyes. Those planks seem so big and obvious to all; how can they even be called specks? Lord, we need Your help to stop comparing ourselves with our ex-spouses and thinking of our sins as somehow less sinful in Your eyes.

Father, guard us against being prideful, bitter, and angry. Soften our hearts, "renew a right spirit" within us, and give us compassion for our ex-spouses (Psalm 51:10, ESV). Please help us be like Christ. It seems impossible at times, but You tell us that we "can do all things through [Christ] who strengthens" us (Philippians 4:13, ESV), and we ask that You would give us strength to forgive. Not because anyone deserves forgiving but because forgiveness gives us the ability to move forward and enables us to be used by You.

God, help us give our children the gift of a forgiving, loving parent. In Jesus' name, amen.

Six

Slashing Tires and Other Thoughts to Take Captive

Whoever is slow to anger is better than the mighty, and he who rules his spirit than he who takes a city.

—Proverbs 16:32, ESV

So we can't avoid the topic of anger—crazy, wanna-do-something-about-it anger that overwhelms and fills us in astonishing ways. I've thought a lot about this. Anger can either spur us on to good deeds or swallow us up in darkness and despair. Some anger is based on righteous indignation, and then there's just plain hate-filled anger based on injury and pain. What has happened to us isn't a small matter that can be overlooked and excused. It has to be dealt with in a realistic and honest way.

There is no way to go through this awful process of abandonment and divorce without a fair share of anger. When your children become the helpless victims of someone else's selfishness, the anger is acute, to say the least. When your covenant partner destroys your relationship, your marriage, and your family, it's impossible to avoid anger. *Angry* doesn't even seem like an appropriate word for the depth of the feeling.

I can't begin to tell you the number of times I wanted to hit, punch, and yell like a barbarian running to battle. I didn't always avoid those things well, although there were no barbarian wails. I tried to express my frustration and anger only in ways that wouldn't scare the neighbors.

But there were also days when I wanted to race over to the other woman's house and rage. Those days were the worst.

When I allowed myself to dwell in the pit of anger, I struggled more than any other time. Lest you think I struggled silently or gently in my anger, let me be honest. I did my fair share of stomping around and slamming things, and I even put a chair leg through the wall once when I put it down with a little too much force and a lot less aim. My kids and I were able to laugh about it because, thankfully, reacting that way was out of character for me. My kids teased me incessantly about it and shared the story with everyone who came by, until I was smart enough to patch and paint the wall.

Needless to say, that outburst stopped me in my tracks. What a waste of energy. My anger sapped me of strength to face the really important tasks before me. No doubt it was a realistic expression of the pain in my life, but I cannot think of a truly helpful or useful purpose for giving full vent to my anger.

It was really easy to become angry. Angry thoughts and actions felt good for about a second . . . maybe a minute . . . okay, days. But I didn't want to waste my time with emotions that didn't help me. I couldn't think of a reason to wallow in anger when I had so much else to deal with daily. I wanted more out of my life. I wanted my children to understand that it was possible to deal with injustice, betrayal, and hurt without falling into that pit. We already struggled with sorrow, frustration, and grief, so why would I want to add another difficult emotion to the mix, if it wasn't absolutely necessary?

The Pit of Anger: Climb Out Fast!

You might be thinking that it's all well and good for me to say, "Don't let yourself become an angry person," but that doesn't explain how to deal with this very real and difficult emotion. And believe me, I know it's a lot easier said than done. During my divorce, I felt as though I had to pray and determine to rise above anger on an ongoing basis. But there are some other practical steps you can take to deal with this overwhelming emotion in constructive and reasonable ways:

1. Surround yourself with people who won't encourage your anger. God gave me grace to not lose myself in my anger. I was definitely angry, irate, and mad as a hornet. I had righteous indignation, yes, but also mama-bear anger and "I'm gonna take you down if I get the chance" anger. However, I didn't act on the latter two. Plenty of people would have assisted in any devious plan I wanted to hatch, but thankfully we resisted the urge.

What my friends did do was give me a safe place to vent. They listened attentively but didn't incite me to more anger. It was important for me to avoid those people who wanted to focus on the anger-inducing aspects of my situation. It would have been entirely too easy to remain furious and want to act on those negative feelings.

Healthy friendships should and will encourage your healing. If you don't feel comfortable sharing with friends or family, or you don't feel that those around you help defuse your anger, seek out a counselor, mentor, or support group. Meeting with a counselor is a great course of action. It's extremely helpful to be able to share with someone who isn't emotionally involved and is trained to offer sound advice.

2. Deal with your anger in appropriate ways. Having a positive attitude was a worthy but difficult objective. The struggle to maintain a peaceful countenance and grace-filled life was constant. I found that dealing with my anger toward my husband and my situation was a major issue, especially during that first year after finding out about the affair. I had to find constructive outlets for my anger. My biggest outlet was my faith. I couldn't have survived with my faith intact, any kind of testimony, and my heart mending if it hadn't been for the Lord sustaining me through His Word, His people, and His presence.

I know it seems almost unbelievable that it's possible to find any relief from the pain and anger of this situation simply by praying and studying Scripture. And yet it made all the difference in my life. I found immense relief in being able to, in a sense, give my cares, concerns, and myriad emotions to God in prayer. The mere act of sharing my deepest thoughts, fears, and hurts with the Lord was a release. I believe He was, and still is, intimately involved in my life and wanted to share my burdens.

Practically speaking, I think that physical activity is also a healthy way of dealing with your anger and offers both physical and emotional benefits. Soon after my husband left, I started running and found that it really helped me focus, breathe, and release some tension.

Another way to deal with anger appropriately is finding some time to invest in something you truly love. This will look different for everyone, but for me, my biggest investment timewise was and still is my kids. Laughing with my children really was the best medicine!

These suggestions may not have scientific support, but I believe they are all helpful in redirecting anger in more positive ways. Focusing on something other than your anger will help you gain a bit more control over this difficult emotion.

3. *Understand that hurt is often at the root of anger.* Most of the time, anger is born of hurt. In abandonment and divorce, most anger is a result of injury and pain. There isn't a deeper hurt I can think of than a spouse's betrayal. Add the hurt of your children to that, and you have a recipe for rage. The fact that my children will have to deal with this betrayal and abandonment to some degree for the rest of their lives was—and still is—devastating to me.

But instead of focusing on the hurt my children had suffered, I began to focus on my children themselves. Instead of reliving the injuries over and over, I made a serious effort to find ways to see the good that was happening around me.

Sometimes that good was as small as a cup of tea on a quiet morning; sometimes it was a special time with one of my children; and sometimes it was a friend who sent a funny card at just the right time. When I chose to focus on my hurt, it was hard to look past it to the beautiful things that were happening in my life. And more importantly, fixing my gaze on my pain would have made it nearly impossible to heal. The ache would never have really stopped if I had kept living it over and over and over again.

Relief from the ache only came when I no longer defined myself by the injury I received. While this has been difficult, it would have been much more difficult to live with the hurt of an unhealed, broken heart.

4. *Forgive.* That's such an itty-bitty word, but golly, it has a whopper of a meaning. There's nothing little or easy about it. We've discussed it at length in the previous chapter, but it can't hurt to hit the highlights again.

In fact, forgiveness is the most important step in your healing. You cannot let go of the anger, pain, and hurt until you let go of your right to be hurt and angry. Forgiveness means you give up something. You no longer seek retribution. You no longer relive the offense or stir up thoughts of anger because you're justified. And, yes, you are justified in your anger, but that doesn't make it healthy for you. The only thing that will alleviate the pain and enable you to begin your journey to healing is letting go of your right to be angry. In some ways, forgiveness is more about you than your offender.

Making the decision to forgive is hard, and following through with it in how you live, react, and interact with your offender is even harder. It doesn't offer instant relief. It's a *process* that begins with a decision to forgive and ends with a healed heart. That heart is yours.

5. *Keep your thoughts under control.* Oh boy, this is a doozy of an issue! We can lose our minds if we brood over things too much. I knew (from personal experience) that if I let myself go to my angry place mentally, there would be no stopping the spiral downward. If I began to think extensively about the effects of betrayal on my family, it would be really easy to start thinking dark thoughts filled with anger, bitterness, and revenge. I had to fight anger by being aware of my thoughts. That sounds odd, but it's really something I needed to do.

I had thoughtless thoughts—autopilot emotional thinking. Wayward, difficult thoughts had to be taken captive. I had to pray, *God, You are able to handle this pain and anger. You can handle my life. I can't.* When it all seemed too much, I tried to rest in His presence. Sometimes that just meant breathing. Sometimes I needed to distract myself in the same way a parent distracts a very young child to avoid danger or injury. I had to recognize the danger my thoughts posed and distract myself by reading Scripture, calling a friend, putting on some music, or focusing on a task before me.

Memorizing Scripture helped, too. One of the verses I memorized was Philippians 4:13: "I can do everything through him who gives me strength."

> *I waited patiently for the LORD; he inclined to me and heard my cry. He drew me up from the pit of destruction, out of the miry bog, and set my feet upon a rock, making my steps secure. He put a new song in my mouth, a song of praise to our God. Many will see and fear, and put their trust in the LORD.*
>
> —PSALM 40:1-3, ESV

Taking my thoughts captive was one of the many things I recognized I couldn't accomplish without God's strength.

6. *Rely on God—not yourself—for the strength to overcome anger.* God is faithful to be all you need, and that includes being the One who lis-

tens to you rage. Go to Him with your anger, with your hurt, with your frustration, with your fear, with your everything. He is able to handle all the emotions of this catastrophe. He won't be offended by your ranting, annoyed by your honesty, or hurt by your questioning. He loves you with an unfailing love.

Isaiah 54:10 says, " 'Though the mountains be shaken and the hills be removed, yet my unfailing love for you will not be shaken nor my covenant of peace be removed,' says the LORD, who has compassion on you." And Psalm 130:7 implores you to "put your hope in the LORD, for with the LORD is unfailing love and with him is full redemption."

What does giving your anger to God look like? I guess what I would say is that you just pray. And you stop and think. Really, *stop*. It's that age-old idea of counting to ten:

1 . . . *I'm so stinkin' angry.*
2 . . . *I can't believe this is happening.*
3 . . . *Why did he do this?*
4 . . . *Oh, God, my children.*
5 . . . *Am I going to survive this?*
6 . . . *Yes.*
7 . . . *Lord, how?*
8 . . . *Lord, You say You are my refuge and strength.*
9 . . . *Lord, show me.*
10 . . . *I trust You, Father.*

Remind yourself who your heavenly Father is. If you are a believer, He is your rock, your fortress, your "ever-present help" in times of trouble (Psalm 46:1). This is a time of trouble; He *will* help. Choose to trust Him even when everything is falling apart. He will provide. He will take care of you. He will be all you need.

I know it sounds too easy in one way and ridiculously difficult in another. "So, He's just gonna handle it all, huh? Cause He's done a fine job up to this point?" (Where is that sarcasm font?) "And how do I just trust Him? What does that look like practically speaking?"

My dear friend, it looks like you living your life and maintaining hope for your future. It is an overarching understanding that this life is tough, and sometimes things turn out very wrong, but you trust that God has a plan in it all. Some of you haven't received child-support payments in months, and bills need to be paid, and trusting God with the practical things of this life seems ridiculous at this point. Some of you haven't seen your children daily since the divorce was finalized, and the pain is intolerable. Some of you have pretty much lost everything. It's a perfectly natural response to question God in the midst of all the destruction.

I know. I understand. I have raised my fist at God when things were falling apart around me. I have voiced difficult questions to Him many times, and sometimes the only answer I received was a sense of peace that surprised me—peace in the middle of pandemonium. We live in a world where things go awry . . . very awry. No one knows this better than you and I.

I can only share what I have found to be true: God is indeed trustworthy, and though His provision in my life hasn't always appeared the way I thought it should, His provision is always good. When I was struggling to make ends meet, God did provide a job for me, as well as friends who made meals, bought groceries, and helped me repair my house and car.

I wish I had an answer for suffering. But I can tell you that although I would have wished to avoid it, I'm thankful for how my pain has changed me for the better. I identify with 2 Corinthians 4:7–9:

> We have this treasure in jars of clay to show that this all-surpassing power is from God and not from us. We are hard pressed on every side, but not crushed; perplexed, but not in despair; persecuted, but not abandoned; struck down, but not destroyed.

That treasure hidden in a jar of clay is the gospel in us. The gospel that shares who Jesus is and what He accomplished by His perfectly lived life, His perfect obedience, and His perfect sacrificial death. My belief that my sins are forgiven because Jesus died for me and that my eternal life is secure because of His resurrection enables me to endure all this life throws at me. Christ is my strength to respond to betrayal with forgiveness, to react to hurt with gentleness and kindness, to find hope when my life is anything but happy, to be thankful even when things are a mess around me.

> *Let us hold unswervingly to the hope we profess, for he who promised is faithful.*
>
> —HEBREWS 10:23

I think we would all prefer a simple to-do list that, when completed, would ensure the fastest and easiest fix for our situations. Unfortunately, I cannot offer a to-do list, but I can offer hope, because Jesus obtained and secured our salvation (Hebrews 6:19).

So when things seem bleak, when you have those dark moments, hold on to the hope you have in Christ. Hold on for dear life. Better days lie ahead.

UNDEFINING ANGER

It's important to remember that allowing anger to be your defining emotion will only hurt you and those you love. You need to allow yourself to feel anger, but please don't let it be the dominant emotion in your life. You have more to live for than revenge and rage. Anger keeps you from moving forward. It feels right and good at times to entertain this beast of an emotion, but it isn't going to help you become a better person or live your life with any joy or peace.

Anger will undoubtedly spill over into other areas of your life. Your children will receive some of the overflow. Your friends and family will see the effects on your relationships with them as you become bitter, critical, and caustic. Your hopes of overcoming the negative influence of this awful situation will diminish significantly if you choose to hold on to anger and hurt.

In the midst of this devastating situation, you are going to be angry. But what are you going to do with your feelings? Are you going to entertain them, relish them, and try to provoke them, or are you going to see them as valid emotions that need to be recognized as such but not encouraged? Give your anger, rage, and hurt to God. He can handle it. He will deal with the situation effectively, graciously, and justly in His time and in His way.

I decided awhile ago that anger wasn't going to mess with me any longer. I was going to fight it head-on every day with faith and forgiveness. And I was going to claim the victory God offered me. Even though life was tumultuous and difficult and sad and frustrating and overwhelming and exhausting, I knew . . . I *knew* that God had it under control. Deep inside my heart, beneath the stormy waters of my life, flowed a lovely current of peace.

Although I struggled with anger, frustration, and questioning why from day one of this trial, I did have an enduring peace. Some days it was weaker than others, but it was always there. I knew with all my heart and mind that God was in control, but I still needed to ask questions and beg for answers. I had to work my way through the process of grieving the loss of my marriage and being furious with my ex-husband. And that was okay. Throughout the whole process, God never left me. And not only did He stay with me; He comforted, strengthened, and guided me through my journey. My relationship with Him became stronger than ever as I learned to abide in Him.

How do we abide in Christ? I believe the answer is living a life of faith. My faith reminded me that God was going to take care of my family. Faith was trusting God—*really* trusting Him. My faith was based on knowing God's character and trusting Him to take care of my family. It was being acquainted with His promises and believing them. It was relying on His leading when I needed to make wise choices. It was experiencing His love and resting in it.

Maybe you're in the middle of your own crisis right now, struggling to work through intense feelings from being betrayed and abandoned. Don't give up! You can trust God with your anger, with your sorrow, with your children, and with your life. God loved me through His words, and the confidence I had in His love gave me the strength to fight my anger and win.

Read these verses aloud and soak in the truth of God's Word. God is faithful and His Word is true!

> The Lord will fight for you, and you have only to be silent.
> (Exodus 14:14, esv) (No small feat for me!)

> He sent from on high, he took me;
>   he drew me out of many waters.
> He rescued me from my strong enemy
>   and from those who hated me,
>   for they were too mighty for me.
> They confronted me in the day of my calamity,
>   but the Lord was my support.
> He brought me out into a broad place;
>   he rescued me, because he delighted in me.
>   (Psalm 18:16–19, esv)

> The Lord is my rock and my fortress and my deliverer,
>   my God, my rock, in whom I take refuge,

my shield, and the horn of my salvation,

    my stronghold and my refuge,

    my savior; you save me from violence.

I call upon the LORD, who is worthy to be praised,

    and I am saved from my enemies. (2 Samuel 22:2–4, ESV)

Dear friend, when your anger is overwhelming, when your heart is broken beyond your ability to repair, please give both to God and allow Him to heal you. This isn't an easy assignment, but it is essential and good. I know because I have lived it!

Father God, You understand all the emotions of our situations—the good, the bad, and the ugly. You understand that we sometimes struggle with getting our thoughts in order. It's so difficult to be "slow to anger" when everything is just plain wrong (James 1:19, ESV).

Lord, sometimes we feel there is nothing we'd rather do than punch holes in the wall. And yet, God, we want to be like You— "quick to listen, slow to speak," "slow to anger, [and] abounding in love" (James 1:19; Exodus 34:6). Sometimes it feels as if we're not able to listen to anything but our own angry thoughts. Father, give us strength to rise above our circumstances, to not be defined by what has happened to us. Help us focus on our healing rather than our hurting.

Lord, this all has to come from You. Change our hearts, God, to be more like Yours. Father, please help us focus on Christ. Please help us understand what it means to abide in Christ (John 15:7). Reveal Yourself to us. Show us that You are indeed our Rock, our Refuge, our Strength, our Comforter, and our Savior, and this battle is Yours and Yours alone (2 Samuel 22:2-4; 2 Chronicles 20:15; 32:8). You will make all things right in the end (Philippians 1:6).

God, be glorified even in this mess.

In Jesus' name, amen.

SEVEN

Killer Legs and Killer Thoughts

And after you have suffered a little while, the God of all grace,
who has called you to his eternal glory in Christ, will himself
restore, confirm, strengthen, and establish you.

—1 PETER 5:10, ESV

This is absolutely the chapter I don't want to write. I don't want to think about this other person, much less devote a chapter to her involvement in my life. At this point it has been a few years since I learned of her existence, and I still struggle with what to do with the feelings I have toward her.

I can't imagine ever wanting to hang out with or get to know her. I struggled with the thought of having to meet her. I kept trying to figure out what we were going to talk about. We certainly weren't going to sit down over coffee and chat about our relationships with my husband—I guess I should say her husband. Ugh. See? No matter how I try to put my godly woman spin on it, I can't figure out how I'm supposed to be.

The reality is that there is nothing normal about a relationship between a wife and a mistress. Maybe one day we'll get to the point of being something other than just acquaintances, but I don't know if I could ever truly be friends with her. Maybe someday, but it would definitely have to be a God thing. To be honest, being friends with her isn't really my priority; I just want to walk through this situation in a way that pleases God, helps my children adjust well, and heals my broken heart.

I have tried from the beginning to not be an angry, bitter, vindictive, abandoned wife. It hasn't been an easy task at times. I've tried not to act based on how I feel but rather on how I want to be. During the first couple of years after my husband left, I felt crazy angry at times, but

Journal entry: I've spent days looking back over all my journals from this tragic time in my life and have discovered that I don't have any entries about the other woman. I probably should go talk to a counselor about that. I wonder why I didn't talk about her at all. I know when my children were preparing to meet her for the first time, I definitely had some thoughts. I was twisted in knots over it. She's not someone I want involved in my children's lives, but I didn't get to say anything about that. I have no say over it. How difficult! I have always had a say in who spends time with my children, and now this person whom I do not respect or even know is going to not only meet my children but have a huge role in their lives. That is so wrong!

In a weird way, I think I've gotten used to it: the idea of this woman being their stepmother. Thankfully, she doesn't really want to be motherly to them—that helps. I just don't know how to feel about it. I know that I have to meet her soon. There are big events coming up—high school graduations, concerts, and so on—I wonder if she's going to want to come. Ugh. Then they will be Mr. and Mrs., and I will be the single divorcée sitting by myself. How pathetic. I hate being divorced. This whole situation from top to bottom is just awful.

I wanted to be calm and peaceful. I felt frustrated, but I wanted to be content. I felt lonely, but I wanted to face these new circumstances successfully. I felt like saying bitter and sarcastic things about my husband and his girlfriend, but I wanted my words to be gentle. I felt like sharing my side of the story with whoever would listen, but I wanted to trust that the truth would prevail.

I felt like acting out against this other woman, but I wanted to be a godly woman. Truthfully, I didn't always want to act in a nice and godly way. There were definitely times when I wanted to be less than stellar. I ranged from wanting to implore her to leave my family alone to wanting to go over to her house and break things. At the start, when I first learned of the affair, I imagined taking all five kids—ages eighteen months, two, eight, twelve, and fifteen—and our one-hundred-pound black Lab and dropping them off on her front porch with a note: "You want my husband? Well, he's a package deal!"

I didn't really want to do that. I just wanted her to understand that there were six other people involved in their drama. Six people who didn't deserve to be part of it at all. My husband and this other woman were acting without regard for anyone but themselves.

During the first few months of this ordeal, one friend advised me to ask to see the other woman and then state my case for why she should leave my husband alone. Another friend told me that plan would only stir up more strife for me and wouldn't change anything. This friend pointed out that the other woman already knew about my five children and me, but that hadn't stopped her from having the affair. I sought additional counsel from my pastor and my counselor. They both felt that it wouldn't be wise to pursue the idea. I followed their advice.

In the past couple of years, I've wished at times that I had at least tried to talk to her, but I believe I made the right decision. I think my friend was correct that this woman was unconcerned with the impact of her actions on my children and me, and there was probably nothing I could have said to change that.

THOUGHTS OUT OF SYNC

In sharing my experience, I don't want to focus so much on the other woman as on the effect she had on my family. Dealing with the introduction of this unwanted individual into my family was confusing and painful. When my husband first left and moved in with her, I was adamant that my children not be exposed to her—at all. We agreed that our children wouldn't be introduced to her until she and my husband had been together for a certain amount of time. My children would also not go to their house while she was there and definitely wouldn't spend the night until they were married.

Thankfully that gave us all time to get used to the idea of this other woman as best we could. She and my ex-husband married about two years after he left. Unfortunately, even after so much time, the two weeks leading up to the wedding were filled with tears and sadness for my children and me. I have to admit that my sadness was over the dashed hopes my children held for reconciliation.

Truthfully, I wish he had married anyone but her. She seems like my archenemy. I'm sure that if I unknowingly sat next to her at a dinner party, we would have nothing in common but would have a delightful conversation nonetheless. I know a lot about what my ex-husband thinks about her. Our counselor even asked him to make a list of everything he knew about her. I wish our counselor had asked him to write a list about me instead.

My ex-husband's list consisted of details about her education, how she liked her coffee, and how he liked playing with her long hair. He mentioned that she was a classic romantic about three times and how she really "got" him all the time. I felt as if I had gone back to junior high school. (Oops, that sounded bitter again.) The list was long, and I wanted to make my own list next to hers:

She loves her pet bird.	I love our five children.
She's romantic.	I faithfully and completely loved him for eighteen years.
She's bonded to him.	I committed my life to him and made and adopted babies with him.
She has a master's degree.	I put him through graduate school.
She has killer legs.	Well, she has me there.

I should stop, because I still get all fired up about that silly list. And that's exactly what it is: a silly list. It doesn't tell the story of our life, our marriage, or our family. It speaks of the deception of sin.

That "blasted list" gets me to my first point, and it is HUGE! We *must* remember this: Our spouse's affair is NOT, NEVER WAS, and NEVER WILL BE about us! It is all about our spouse's issues, sins, and attitudes! I'm not saying there aren't things we could have done better in our marriages, but there is *never* anything that makes adultery a proper response. Never!

I would have done anything to get my husband to stay—changed my look or my body, moved, remodeled, stopped homeschooling, gone to work, whatever. He knew that. It didn't matter, because, ultimately, it wasn't about me. It wasn't even about her and the carefree existence without responsibility or accountability that she offered him. It was about him and his issues alone.

Thoughts on Motherhood
and Stepmotherhood

It's amazing to me that after so many years, I still haven't met this woman who has played such a pivotal role in my family. She doesn't attend any of my children's school or sporting events, and she is generally uninvolved in their lives. Most often when my ex-husband has our children, she isn't around. I consider that a blessing. I like to think that maybe she doesn't get involved with our children as a kindness to me, but that's probably just me with my rose-colored glasses on.

Five children can be overwhelming, and maybe she just wanted my husband and not the package deal. Personally, I think the package deal was quite a wonderful arrangement! I have mentioned to my ex-husband that I'd be willing to meet her, but nothing has happened as of yet, and that was quite awhile ago. My kids don't talk about her much, and out of love for them, I don't ask questions. I know it makes them uncomfortable to talk about her with me, and I get that. As curious as I am, I've been able to keep my nosiness to a minimum.

Sometimes I imagine that we'll meet and get along just fine, be able to talk about my children, and get past all this stuff. Maybe God would even use me to tell her about Him. I've been praying about what meeting her would look like, where we would meet, and what we would talk about. I believe that God has brought me to a place where I would truly be okay with meeting her. Although as much as I say that and mean it, I suspect it will be difficult to get past the tension between us.

The biggest tension is her role as a stepmom. It's one thing to deal with her intrusion in my life, but dealing with her relationship with my children is a whole other thing—a whole other unpleasant thing. I know that my teenagers, at least to some degree, understand the dynamics of the relationships. And by that I mean they know the roles people have played in the explosion of our family. Unfortunately, that information was out of my hands before I even grasped it firmly myself.

My little girls don't really understand who this woman is and will probably eventually become completely enamored with this fun person who only appears in their lives occasionally. My middle son is conflicted because this woman he wanted to dislike is likable. My job is to make sure my children don't feel as if they are being disloyal to me just because they like their dad's new wife. No easy task to be sure, but I'm determined to make this as easy as possible for my children, even if it's exceedingly difficult for me.

I'm currently dealing with a few issues regarding this woman's role as my children's stepmother. First of all, I'm jealous of my time with them and don't want to share them with her. Second, she isn't the type of woman I would ever choose to be an influence in my children's lives. Third, I want my children to like me best of all. Okay, in all honesty, that's probably the main one.

She deals with the issues of caring for five children for maybe a couple of hours every once in a while and can offer a fun and undisciplined environment, whereas I need to be Mom. Mom, who makes them do chores, sets schedules, puts them to bed, and disciplines them when they are disobedient. But I'm also Mom who loves them unabashedly, who holds them daily, prays for them, makes their meals, does their seven million loads of laundry, encourages them, helps them with their homework, and faces life with them when it's challenging, scary, and difficult, or even fun, silly, and crazy. And while all of that takes work, to me, being Mom is the greatest blessing of my life.

Thoughts About Me—Who I Am and Whose I Am

So, this is what I want you to do. I want you to quit putting that other person on a pedestal. Take him or her off that perch, because this person absolutely doesn't deserve to be there. Anyone who is willing to play a leading role in the destruction of a family, a marriage, and another human being is no one to think highly of—even if she does have killer legs.

Next, I want you to really take a look at yourself, your amazing survivor self. Remind yourself of who you are or can be in Christ. When my oldest was a little boy, I taught his Sunday school class, and we memorized this verse: "How great is the love the Father has lavished on us, that we should be called children of God! And that is what we are!" (1 John 3:1).

I always thought that was one of the best verses to memorize. That word *lavished* is such a wonderful description of how God pours His love on us. It isn't a small amount, just enough to get us through the day. It isn't a decent amount that comforts us when things go badly. He gives us limitless love. There is no end to His love for us.

The chapter goes on to say that we know this is love because "Jesus Christ laid down his life for us" (verse 16). My friend, God doesn't just say He loves you; He demonstrated that love when, on the cross, He rescued you from your sin: "God shows his love for us in that while we were still sinners, Christ died for us" (Romans 5:8, ESV). How valuable you are in His sight!

God knows you and loves you. "Why, even the hairs of your head are all numbered. [So] fear not; you are of more value than many sparrows" (Luke 12:7, ESV). To all of us who believe in His name, "he gave the right to become children of God" (John 1:12). You are chosen, rescued, and forgiven because of Jesus' sacrifice on the cross (Galatians 3:13; 1 Peter 2:9–10).

I long for us all to understand what Jesus has done for us. We didn't do anything worthy of His good opinion. And yet Christ still died for us. He knew our tendencies, our temptations, and our sins, and He still loved us enough to die for us. He *still* loves us enough to die for us. And He didn't choose us just because we were all cute and adorable. He chose us when we were all dirty, smelly, and rebellious. He loves us even when we feel unlovable.

Allow Him to "quiet you with his love" (Zephaniah 3:17), to calm your anxious thoughts, and to assure you that regardless of how you're feeling or what you're going through at this moment, you are dearly loved.

Understanding who I am and whose I am enables me to grasp the magnitude of that sacrifice and the awesome and wondrous ramifications it has on my life. As a child of God, forgiven and redeemed, I must remind myself that there is no condemnation, period (Romans 8:1). First John 3:19–21 says, "By this we shall know that we are of the truth and reassure our heart before him; for whenever our heart condemns us, God is greater than our heart, and he knows everything. Beloved, if our heart does not condemn us, we have confidence before God" (ESV).

> *The LORD your God is with you, he is mighty to save. He will take great delight in you, he will quiet you with his love, he will rejoice over you with singing.*
>
> —ZEPHANIAH 3:17

You know what I love about those verses? God tells us that He knows everything, and He still doesn't condemn us! I'm thinking that if God knows everything, and that includes *everything* about us, and He still doesn't condemn us, we have no right to do it ourselves. So when you want to compare yourself to this other person, when you can only see your deficiencies, inadequacies, and mistakes, please, oh please, remember that. You are chosen and loved not because of anything you did or didn't do but simply because God is who He is.

Before we go any further, there is something else I want you to do, because in the end it will bless you. If you can bring yourself to do it—I haven't been as successful at this as I'd like—pray for the other person. I believe that through the process of prayer, God will soften your heart and heal some of the broken and cracked places. Pray that God would change that other person's heart. I honestly wish I had prayed for my replacement more; it was definitely a stumbling block for me. I did at the beginning. Before my ex-husband started living with her, it was easier for me to pray for her.

When there was hope for reconciliation, I could pray. How selfish was that! I'm seeing now that maybe the reason it was easier to remember to pray for her back then was because it was in my best interests for her to "come to her senses." I now pray for not only my ex-husband but also for his wife. And I pray with a true desire for them to know His peace, true joy, and real love.

STRONG AND COURAGEOUS THOUGHTS

The verses that spoke to me deeply during my divorce, and still do, were those that spoke of who God was to me:

> I will not leave you or forsake you. Be strong and courageous. . . .
> Have I not commanded you? Be strong and courageous. Do not be
> frightened, and do not be dismayed, for the LORD your God is with
> you wherever you go. (Joshua 1:5–6, 9, ESV)

Though I felt forgotten, forsaken, and abandoned by my ex-spouse, the truth is that I am not and never will be forgotten, forsaken, or abandoned by the One who knows me best.

Isaiah 54:5–6 reminded me that God would be my husband:

> For your Maker is your husband, the LORD of hosts is his name; and
> the Holy One of Israel is your Redeemer, the God of the whole earth
> he is called. For the LORD has called you like a wife deserted and

grieved in spirit, like a wife of youth when she is cast off, says your God. (ESV)

Sweet friend, you can be strong and courageous because you are His. You are so much more than an abandoned spouse—*so* much more. No matter who or what your spouse chooses over you, know this: You are loved beyond measure by your heavenly Father. You are fearfully and wonderfully made and deeply and unconditionally loved. Don't dwell on comparisons. God designed you like an exquisite tapestry (Ephesians 2:13). He knows everything about you and still loves you with an everlasting, unconditional, passionate love—killer legs or not.

Dearest Father, please help us find our identity in Christ. Lord, it's such a struggle to deal with the unwanted people You have allowed into our lives. We cannot imagine ever being able to truly love them, but You have called us to love our enemies and pray for those who hurt us (Matthew 5:44).

Lord, it feels impossible to even be civil at times. Father, please use us to show them Your love even if that just means doing them no verbal harm. Thank You that You have freed us from all condemnation, even condemning ourselves. Thank You that we have grace and love and hope and purpose because of Jesus. Lord, we are comforted by Your promise to never leave us or forsake us (Matthew 28:20; Hebrews 13:5). Oh, Father, please help us keep our focus on Jesus. Please be glorified in our lives.

In Jesus' name, amen.

EIGHT

Unexpected Blessings

I was pushed back and about to fall, but the LORD helped me. The LORD is my strength and my song; he has become my salvation.

—PSALM 118:13–14

When I first started down this difficult path, I lived with a strong and steady hope that God was going to do something amazing. He did, but as is usually the case, it wasn't what I expected. I've shared that the second year was the most difficult in many ways, maybe because the numbness had worn off. All of a sudden, I realized I was living my "new normal," and I didn't like it at all. I remember praying, *Lord, this is where You have us? This can't really be where You want us. I thought something would happen and change everything for the better.* I don't know exactly what my definition of *better* was, but I thought life shouldn't be so tough.

There wasn't any place in my life where something wasn't at least slightly askew. But in the midst of my fussing, I needed to remember the fact that my children and I were happy together, healthy, and still in our home. That in itself was pretty amazing! I really thought we might be living with friends and barely hanging on financially, emotionally, and spiritually.

Thankfully, and not surprisingly, God's plan was to provide for and protect my children and me. I could write a book about all the ways He has provided for me, not only in practical, necessary ways, but also in completely frivolous, unexpected, and lovely ways.

Wait a minute! I *am* writing that book! So let me share some of the ways my God loved on me and mine through the people He placed in our lives:

- People watched my children for me when I needed to work or just have a minute to rest.
- People dropped off meals and gift cards randomly.
- My church bought me a freezer, and my friends filled it.
- Someone left an Advent basket on my front porch. The basket was filled with a gift for every day of the Advent season. It blessed me so much. The notes attached to the gifts were humorous and/or inspiring, and each was perfect for the day I opened it.
- Friends loaned me their van when I was trying to sell my car (and its car payment), so my car could stay pristine. That was such a sacrificial thing to do, considering the number and ages of my children!
- A lady from church planted flowers in my front-step flower-pots, which had been empty for quite a while.
- My church had a workday at my house and completed everything on my repair list. I had so many little and big issues I couldn't or didn't know how to address. They replaced broken door handles and hinges, fixed holes in the floor, planted trees, and dug a vegetable garden, and so many other things.
- A couple of ladies at church brought my children and me clothes whenever they had a chance. Actually, they still do, and I love it!
- People came over, grabbed my laundry, and took it home to wash and dry. Friends took one or more of my children for the day. Friends helped me sort clothing, organize toys, plan meals, clean things, perform bedtime rituals. And the list goes on and on and on.

- One friend came over every night for a week to help me stay strong with a plan so my little girls would establish a better bedtime routine.
- Friends spent almost every day with me for almost three weeks to help me get my home better organized.
- One friend always welcomed my "twister sisters" (Elizabeth and Allison) when I wanted to take the big kids out for something special.

For about six months, a day didn't go by without someone showing up at my door to visit or drop off something. I was in awe of God's provision through His people. I still am. A couple of years ago, I would have been reticent to accept any assistance from someone else, but no longer. I'm needy and I know it. Whenever possible, I try to bless others in return. I want to seize any opportunities God provides for me to give or receive!

My children have been blessed to see our friends and family reach out to us in very practical ways. They are

May the God of hope fill you with all joy and peace as you trust in him, so that you may overflow with hope by the power of the Holy Spirit.

—ROMANS 15:13

learning how to comfort and how to be comforted. And they are hopefully developing servants' hearts as they are being served.

I'm also praying that I will be a better woman, mother, and friend because I know the blessing of being cared for and loved. There is something wonderful about someone dropping off dinner unexpectedly. There is something simply beautiful about someone jumping in to help with the practical stuff of daily life. I'm so looking forward to the day when I can be the one blessing others instead of the one receiving all the blessings! I'm determined to be the kind of person who serves others with love, kindness, and for God's glory (1 Peter 4:10–11).

Journal entry: Father, today while I was surrounded with friends who were helping me organize my home, I had a moment of joy. It was so nice to feel it—I've been living in such a place of pain that joy has seemed almost nonexistent. I looked at each of them working diligently—each has a ton of things they need to do at their homes, and yet they are spending their time here with me. I'm in awe of their love. They keep me busy so my mind doesn't dwell on the tragedy of my life.

Thank You for all the laughter. My friends keep me laughing even through my tears. One of my friends always says the funniest things about my situation . . . it kind of helps for someone to say the obvious stuff. It's nice to hear someone say the things I'm thinking but trying not to say. That's probably bad on some level, but all these emotions are hard to handle. . . .

Having my friends surround me has been more of a blessing than I could ever have thought. It has been nice to have normal conversations while we organize and toss. It has even been nice to be teased about the number of craft supplies I have in the basement—especially since I'm not really that crafty. It has made all the difference to have something to look forward to each day . . . time with dear friends. I believe my children are blessed by the activity too. They are jumping into the organizational fray and even smiling a fair amount.

Lord, thank You for simple pleasures . . . beautiful friends . . . and joy in sorrow.

FAITH IN THE FACE OF THIS LIFE

I began to realize that my faith and obedience had been based very much on the blessings I had hoped to receive from God. I'd been obeying so that I would always be in God's perfect will *so that* God, in turn, would do great things in my life, which would enable me to do great things to please Him. I wanted my life to justify a big ole reward from the Lord. Unfortunately, I was a tad off base in my thinking. The tricky thing about a faith based on receiving good things is when things fall apart—and they will—faith tends to falter.

The motivation of my faith must be my love for Jesus. If I do all things because God is the love of my life, my faith won't be altered by messy and painful things. I'll still be able to trust God and know that He has a good plan for my life, which He will bring to completion (Philippians 1:6). I will be confident in who He is and what He says. I will trust and obey God not because I'm hoping for some wonderful blessing but because I love Him!

I can tend toward a faith that assumes that God is always going to teach me a lesson or let me learn the hard way. Fortunately, that isn't the God I love and serve. He will use circumstances to grow me, but I don't believe He's waiting for me to pray some unsuspecting prayer that allows Him to slam me with a character lesson. Even greater than this realization is the knowledge that as passionate as I want to be about Jesus, He is infinitely more passionate about me. He loves me beyond my imagining. What a blessed realization in the midst of my trials.

The fact is, though, that things changed spiritually for me as my life circumstances changed. My healing was a process, and it often felt like two steps forward and seventy-five back. The tasks became more demanding, and my hold on the Lord loosened. I went from being the woman I had always wanted to be—a prayer warrior, armed to the teeth with the Word, battling on my knees day and night, overflowing with hope—to a fatigued single parent of five working full-time, falling to my knees in exhaustion every night, overflowing with sorrow and fear. How did that happen? My focus changed.

Those God-sized tasks gave way to the smaller tasks of daily living that I thought I could handle all by myself, and I took my eyes off the Lord. When I started focusing only on my life and not the hope and love I had in the Lord, I began to lose heart. I saw no end to the life I was in. My hope began to fade. My prayer life consisted of, *Seriously, God? This is Your great plan for my life?* and *This is Your best for my children and me?*

I didn't lose my faith or even stop trusting God. I just really didn't understand. There are things I still don't understand. But what I have discovered is that maybe understanding *why* isn't as important as how I move forward in my new circumstances. Changing the whole way I approached the Lord, faith, and obedience was challenging. I restarted my daily habit of reading God's Word so I could obey Him for the right reasons and in the right way. I wanted to live passionately for Him even though (and I'm just being real with you) the thing I felt most passionate about at that moment was getting more sleep. But I wanted to obey with my heart in the right place, not simply to get a reward in the end.

> *Praise be to the God and Father of our Lord Jesus Christ, the Father of compassion and the God of all comfort, who comforts us in all our troubles, so that we can comfort those in any trouble with the comfort we ourselves have received from God.*
>
> —2 Corinthians 1:3–4

God gave me great hope for the future—actually, for each day I was living. I was and still am hopeful of what God is going to do as He takes what I have been through and what I have lost and converts it into something brilliant (Joel 2:25–27). It was very difficult to accept that my marriage was over, especially as a Christian. I had covenanted with God to stick it out through thick and thin, sickness and health, good and bad. Divorce wasn't in my life plan. (I seriously doubt many people put that into their life plan.) And although I had to work through my sense of being a failure, I eventually allowed myself to grasp that I had indeed succeeded in traversing the catastrophe of divorce with dignity, strength, and my faith firmly intact.

I can look back and see that God has been more than faithful and kind to my children and me. I can look at my life and see His care so evidently. I'll admit there are more nights than I can count when I've begged God to enable my children to sleep through the night, because I'm pretty sure I haven't hit REM sleep in years. And I wish I knew why God has allowed so very many things to go wrong with my house. My basement has been wet more than dry. In fact, recently it flooded for the tenth time *this year*. One more time, and I'm turning my house into a water park and charging admission.

I've also learned that it is within my ability to approach all those little annoyances with humor. Seriously—or maybe I should say not seriously—I can find some humor in every situation if I look hard enough. I'm pretty sure my life could be a successful sitcom or dramedy, depending on the day. This divorced, single-parent life is challenging and chaotic, but it's also rewarding and full of joyful moments.

Those are the moments I remember at night as I lie in bed reviewing the day. It would be easy to reflect on every day and despair; each day has its challenges. Fortunately, I trust that God is using this nutty life to fashion me into a strong, grace-filled woman, inside and out. My job is to approach each day with a firm understanding that God loves me no matter what, that He cares about all the little things that happen throughout the day, and He will use all of it for something good.

This Life and Its Unexpected Gifts

We'd all probably change our circumstances in some way if we could—maybe in every way. Although it wouldn't be easy to transform our lives into what we want them to be, God can transform us into the parents and people we *need* to be to live this life successfully.

I've seen Him work beautiful things in my children's lives. Last year Zachary went on a missions trip to Peru to work with orphan boys. When he returned, he said his favorite part was being with the boys—playing soccer, working on projects, and just hanging out. Weekly Zach goes to a home for disabled adults and just visits. I believe God has blessed my son with a heart for those who have suffered and experienced loss.

He's a very busy teenager with school, a job, activities, sports, and a single mom who often needs his help, but he makes time to reach out to others. I see that my son has developed gentleness and a servant's heart for those who are hurting. I believe much of that is because he has seen it modeled by our friends and family as they have ministered to us. I also believe he has grown up to be a responsible and accountable young man who is stronger in his faith because of the challenges our family has endured. To me, this is a picture of God making something beautiful out of a tragic situation.

As I mentioned earlier, Emma and I have a very close relationship, even as she works through the natural changes of growing up. God has given us a love for each other that I believe has been strengthened through adversity survived together. She is kind and loving toward me, values my opinion, and confides easily in me. I don't know if this would have been our relationship were it not for what we have been through. I believe God is using our relationship to strengthen her and inspire her to live in a way that pleases God and blesses others.

Peter wants to save the world. He longs to champion the cause of all the little guys out there. He wants to grow up and serve in the military so that he can rescue people. God has taken this tender young man and given him a warrior's heart. He's often the one standing up for the child who is being picked on or sharing his faith with the kid who is causing all the trouble. He is bold with his faith and strong in his commitment. I see God taking the fears he had when his father left and turning them into strengths.

It's not easy to understand or accept that God will use all the garbage in our lives to fashion something lovely and good. I've complained many times to Him for not making things better in a timelier manner. I've wondered why He didn't use a different means of strengthening us. I've struggled with the long-term repercussions on me and my children because of this, *but* I'm comforted when I take a moment to observe that my family is doing quite well. When I look at who my children are becoming, I'm amazed.

So here I am: single, divorced, and exhausted. I have to be brutally honest; this is *so* not where I thought I would be at this point in my life. Being single in my forties is not ideal. But even though my fairy-tale glass slipper was shattered before I got to the ball, my carriage turned into a pumpkin at 10:00 PM, and my prince was certainly no prince, I'm doing all right.

I have a better Prince who has truly rescued me. He might not hold me tight at night and whisper sweet words in my ear, but His presence is comforting and His words are encouraging and true. My fairy tale might not have followed the story line I had hoped for, but I know that the ending is going to be sweet! I'm excited to see what God is going to continue to do in my life and the lives of my children.

Father, sometimes we just want to cry for all the things we have to deal with on a daily basis. We want to be the best people and parents we can be, but sometimes we feel so defeated by our situations and circumstances. We want to be godly regardless of the mess around us. Lord, we trust that You are going to use all the difficult things in our days, in our lives, to make us into the people You designed us to be, but it just feels so impossible sometimes. Oh, Father, we desperately want rest and peace, but they seem unattainable right now. Please help us grasp the peace that "surpasses all understanding," which will guard our hearts and minds in Christ Jesus (Philippians 4:7, ESV).

Thank You for the homes that keep our children secure and warm. Thank You for our cars, even when they make funny noises. Thank You for our children, who may drive us crazy at times but whom we love dearly. Father, we can't imagine our lives without them. We are indeed blessed. Lord, forgive us when we lose sight of that. Oh, Father, You are so good to us. Thank You.

In Jesus' name, amen.

NINE

24/7 Doesn't Begin to Describe Single Parenting

If the LORD had not been my help, my soul would soon have lived in the land of silence. When I thought, "My foot slips," your steadfast love, O LORD, held me up. When the cares of my heart are many, your consolations cheer my soul.

—PSALM 94:17–19, ESV

Single parenting stinks.

I feel as if I could leave it at that, and this chapter would be complete. Single parenting is the most difficult thing I've ever done by a long shot. You probably get that. But in some unexpected ways, it's also the most rewarding. Parenting my children alone has stretched me in every direction—physically, emotionally, spiritually, and mentally. At times I'm tired and tearful, but I've learned to push through. One of my friends and I joke about putting our big-girl pants on to face life's challenges. My big-girl pants are way bigger than I'd like, but I'm putting them on faithfully.

I'm growing up into my circumstances in a sense. I'm learning about myself in the process. Some of the things I see are rather disappointing, but other things are surprisingly good. There are very real issues I must face head-on as I deal with the aftermath of adultery and divorce and the impact on my children and me. But each challenge I face and conquer is gratifying. It might be terribly hard, but I'm becoming a woman and mother who is strong and fearless, and whose big-girl pants are beginning to fit quite well!

My best mom vision for my family is coming in fits and starts. I want us to be happy, healthy, and a bit more organized. Most of the time, we're a chaotic, loud, emotional, crazy, loving bunch of people. I think we have happy down—at least most of the time—and we're working on healthy. But organized? It seems like as soon as I get one thing dealt with, another thing starts up.

At the moment, the issue is an inability for all of us to rest at night . . . particularly the little people. I don't think I'll have organizational success until I can think clearly, and that means I need some serious sleep. Unfortunately, the defining word of my single parenting experience so far is *exhaustion*. As hard as I try, I cannot get a good night's sleep. I find myself staying up late at night to hang out with my big kids, sleeping in fits and starts throughout the night, and getting up early with my little kids. Even if I go to bed at a reasonable hour (and that is completely relative), the "Wake Momma up!" options are limitless. I think I'm destined to be deliriously tired. In fact, we are all just plain tired. There's simply too much to do!

The bedtime routines alone take forever—and I'm not referring to my facial regimen. I'm referring to spending quality time with each of my children. It takes hours—really, hours. When the kids are finally settled in bed, my night still goes on—lunches, laundry, dishes, and general mom chores. My goal has become to be in bed before it's tomorrow.

Unfortunately, I also have to deal with the middle-of-the-night mommy issues that arise—nightmares and headaches and little people wandering the halls. I really want to be a sweet, patient, loving mommy 24/7. It's just really, really hard. I joke that I thought I'd be well rested by this stage of my life!

The beauty of it is that even in the midst of my ridiculously not-well-rested life, I've found clarity—the realization of what is truly important. Besides, I've decided that sleep is overrated. Sure, it's good to keep the wrinkles away, the joints from aching, and the head from spinning, but I've found that lots of things are funnier when you're exhausted!

God gives me grace to face each day with a new determination to love and live well. So I'll be a little more tired and a little less organized, but I'll also laugh more and enjoy my children regardless of their middle-of-the-night antics. And I'll remember that although it seems inconceivable, this is a season I might actually miss someday!

Loving My Lovable and Not-So-Lovable Children

I chuckle often about the number and ages of my children. It's crazy that I'm a single mom of five children. Five! That's totally nuts! And with basically a child in every stage of development, I think I should be giving lectures on parenting. Fortunately for you, at the moment I'm too busy doing it to tell anyone how to parent! I must say that my children are wonderful. They really are. There are moments each day when I look at them and my heart just wants to burst from love and thankfulness. My children are the best things that ever happened to me. But . . . there are other moments when I just want to box them all up, put them on the front porch, and call UPS. So far I have refrained.

There are days when I can't believe how difficult it is to be a good mom. There was a night—well, actually, almost every night is like this—when I had the sweetest time preparing my three youngest children for bed. I prayed with them, snuggled them under their covers, and kissed them each goodnight. Unfortunately, two hours later the night had digressed. Let's just say I hope I was hormonal, because otherwise I'm losing the rest of my mind. The first half left a long time ago.

After a less-than-stellar mom moment of yelling at my children, who were chatting instead of snoring, I plopped down with a book I had been reading. It was about finding joy and giving thanks in all of life's circumstances. I instantly thought, *Really? This is the book I chose to read? I don't want to find joy. My kids are stinkers and my life is tough and I want to wallow!*

But I read on, and God reminded me through the pages of that book that joy isn't about how I feel or how well my life is going. It's about loving God. There I sat feeling just awful that my good day had deteriorated into disaster. We'd all been persnickety. I really should have been setting the example, and I hadn't. My speech hadn't been gracious or encouraging. It had been fussy, mean, and loud.

I really felt I needed to apologize, but I didn't want to start them chatting again. And then all of a sudden, three little people sheepishly appeared. "Mama, we are so sorry." Humbled doesn't begin to describe how I felt. Thankful and apologetic, I welcomed them all into my arms. And I realized once again, no matter how aggravating they all are, I'm so very thankful for my children, and I love them fervently. And, thank the Lord, no matter how grumpy and impatient I am, my children still love me, too!

Forgiveness is a beautiful thing offered daily at our house. My kids offer so much grace to me. I have days when I feel as if my head might explode and fire might start shooting from my ears, but I'm honest. I warn them when they need to take cover. I'm also forthcoming with my requests for forgiveness. I ask for it a lot. Frankly, I'm getting tired of hearing myself ask for it. I'm sure they are, too. At least they're learning the value of forgiving "seventy-seven times" (Matthew 18:21–22).

I figure there is a teachable moment, or a thousand teachable moments, in each day when surviving a tragedy. I'm trying to teach my children to be forgiving, kind, and understanding people. I try to present the real me to them, but the challenge is that there's a fine line between being completely honest with my children and being real enough so that they aren't bewildered and confused by my emotions and actions.

When things were at their worst during this whole ordeal, my children recognized that it was very difficult for me. I wanted them to see me succeed, but there were good days and rough days. I've endeavored to show my children that there's strength to be gained in the struggle. I've made it my mission to be honest about difficult or sad times without weeping on their shoulders.

I want them to know I do feel things—that I care—but I don't want

Journal entry: Lord, five kids? And me a single parent? I'm so tired. Father, why does it have to be this way? It is so hard. I wasn't made to be both Mom and Dad. I'm not good at it. Being Mom was hard enough; now I have to be Dad, too. I can't even think straight anymore. Everyone has so many needs, so many wants, so many issues. I think I have the most.

I love all my children so much. I have all these things I want to do with them, things I want to accomplish for them, ways I want to bless them. But, Father, I can't seem to get one of these things done well. I feel like such a failure. I don't want to just be surviving single parenthood; I want to be thriving. Each morning I wake up hopeful for the day ahead, and each night I go to bed exhausted and disappointed that I didn't do better. My to-do list seems endless. I feel like a hamster on a wheel. Lord, please help me find balance. Please help me let go of what I need to let go of and hold on dearly to what's most important.

to overwhelm them with my emotions. I have to be careful to keep my complaining to a minimum, my frustration with their father completely hidden, and my sorrow only slightly visible. My need to talk and share and vent cannot ever be directed at my children. It's important that I allow them to talk to me, share with me, and vent to me, but we cannot have a reciprocal relationship. I cannot stress this enough for any single parent who is navigating the stormy seas of divorce.

CLUMSY GRACE

I'm working on a shoestring budget of emotional energy. I don't have any to spare for unnecessary drama. This state of life makes it difficult to deal with the natural, naughty antics of preschoolers, the exploits of an upper-elementary-aged boy, and the angst of teenagers. Each day there are flashes of pain that make my heart hurt and moments of laughter that make my stomach ache. Sometimes my life seems absurd, and the only proper response is laughter. It's either that or weep uncontrollably!

Recently, while I was just ten feet away making dinner, my two little girls decorated our guinea pig with glitter, glue, and feathers. I'm still not sure how I didn't catch on to what was happening. After my initial shock abated, we all got a good laugh. Although I'm certain Blaster, the guinea pig, was not amused.

Then there are days when my children can't say a kind word to one another. Those are heartbreaking days for me. I long for my children to love each other and treat each other kindly. It's all normal, natural stuff, but sometimes it's overwhelming when you are the only parent to referee, discipline, and encourage.

I believe God is showing me that despite these ridiculous circumstances, He won't just help me survive; He will also strengthen me for all that lies ahead in my life. He will give me grace to handle each challenge,

whether it's my oldest starting college and two youngest starting kinder-
garten in the fall or the unknown future that will very likely involve me
going through menopause while my youngest daughters go through pu-
berty. Now *that's* a scary thought!

There are many things that could cause me to fear, but I am confident
that God isn't going to abandon me now or in the future. My hope is secure that He will indeed bring good out of all this. And part of that good
is my becoming a stronger and more faithful woman and mother. I don't
always do this gracefully. I'm trying, but as my neighbors can attest, there
are definitely days when the noise and chaos coming from our end of the
cul-de-sac are extremely difficult to ignore.

Decision-Making for the Indecisive

I think much of what I struggle with as a single mom I would probably
struggle with as a married mom. Things are just intensified now. If you're
a single parent, you can probably understand this. Everything seems so
much more crushing because I'm alone in the parenting decisions, dilemmas, and dynamics.

There isn't a dad to balance me on emotional or stressed-out days.
There isn't a dad to enable me to spend time with only one or two children at a time. There isn't a dad who can take over so I can regroup alone
in my bedroom. I can try to do that, but someone always ends up crying
downstairs if I hide upstairs.

Although sometimes I am physically tired and emotionally drained,
I believe the mental fatigue is what really gets me. I get weary of trying
to figure out all the details, of having to make all the decisions, and of
second-guessing myself. It's exhausting.

I've figured out a few guidelines that have helped me with the decision-making dilemma. When I started writing them down, I realized

that God had been leading me to do just what His Word says to do. How blessed I am to have a God who leads me by His Word even before I'm looking for the answers in it! I hope you'll find these guidelines helpful.

1. Pray and study God's Word. When you're facing a decision, spend time in prayer and in God's Word. There are a couple of verses in Psalm 25 that should be my mantra: "Show me your ways, O LORD, teach me your paths; guide me in your truth and teach me, for you are God my Savior, and my hope is in you all day long" (Psalm 25:4–5). I have had some big, looming decisions regarding education for my children. None of these decisions has been straightforward. There have been so many variables that my head can't even keep track of them all.

One day I was feeling particularly overwhelmed by the whole process while I was unloading the dryer. I had to stop what I was doing and just pray. I asked God to please make it very clear what I should do about my children's education. I asked if I had missed something He was trying to show me, and if He could please show me again. I prayed that He would not only direct my path but that His light would shine brightly enough that I could see the next step to take. He provided some very knowledgeable people to talk with that day. All were empathetic and willing to listen. It was helpful to talk through issues and hear what others thought.

The biggest thing God revealed to me as I sought Him that day was that it was a great opportunity to teach my daughter Emma and my son Peter about the power of prayer. So we covenanted with each other to pray nightly for God to show us His plan. We also prayed for peace and unity with regard to the decision. They both knew the decision was ultimately mine to make, but they seemed grateful and a little excited to take part in the process. I prayed that it would also equip them to be better decision makers.

2. Research and converse. Before making a major decision, take time to do your homework and consult with others who can give you good advice. I generally follow a three-step process. First, I seek additional information from any sources I can find, and I talk to people. I try to discuss things with people I know hold the same values I do. Proverbs 15:22 says, "Plans fail for lack of counsel, but with many advisers they succeed," and Proverbs 20:18 says, "Make plans by seeking advice." That confirms to me that seeking advice is a good thing.

There are people in my life who have life wisdom I don't have, who have worked through similar decisions, and who have come to good conclusions. It's to my benefit to share my questions, dilemmas, and looming decisions with them.

Next, when facing a decision, I investigate things that might impact that decision. And finally, I evaluate all the information I've received and prayerfully make my decision.

I mentioned that I recently had some big educational decisions to make. My schooling dilemma presented three options: public school, Christian school, or homeschool. There were financial issues, moral issues, academic quality issues, social issues, and stress issues associated with each. I spoke with representatives of all three options, and I researched what was offered by each. I compiled all my data and prayed over it, hoping that God would show me exactly what was best for each of my children.

The process took much longer than I imagined it would. I kept wondering if the Lord had revealed the answer to me and I'd missed it. Was I ignoring His leading because it wasn't what I really wanted? Was I being stubborn? I had to stop and take a break from all my questions. I had to be still for a minute and look at all that I had learned.

I came to realize that God wasn't going to send me a lightning bolt with a memo attached containing explicit directions for my children's education. God doesn't always give obvious answers, but I believe that He gives wisdom and knowledge so that we are well equipped to confidently make the decisions we need to make in our lives.

3. Trust and relax. That means no stressing! I want to put a big LOL (laugh out loud) here because I'm absolutely no good at not stressing. I overanalyze things and worry about what will happen if I do one thing or don't do another thing. I could drive myself absolutely nuts with all my what-ifs and whys and wondering *Was that right?* I'm quite silly about it. This is another one of those times where I have to, in a sense, let go and let God.

I'm reminded in Psalm 139 that no matter where I am, God will guide me: "If I rise on the wings of the dawn, if I settle on the far side of the sea, even there your hand will guide me, your right hand will hold me fast" (verses 9–10). It's important that I tell myself all the things I tend to tell other people. I'm always telling people to trust God and believe that what He says He will do, He will in fact do. He says He will give me wisdom, knowledge, and understanding if I ask for it and seek it (Proverbs 2:6; James 1:5).

I'm definitely asking—*begging* might be a better word—and seeking. And I know that at just the right time, God will show me what to do. One of my favorite verses is Isaiah 40:11: "He tends his flock like a shepherd: He gathers the lambs in his arms and carries them close to his heart; he gently leads those that have young."

What a beautiful picture for those of us who aren't held often! The Lord has gathered us in His arms and is holding us close to His heart and gently leading us to our destinations.

4. Make a decision! Sometimes you just have to make a decision. I have to remind myself that not every decision is a moral one. By that I mean there isn't something in the Bible that says I have to send my children to a Christian school for them to become godly people. I tend to make everything a life-or-death decision. But I believe that sometimes God just wants me to use the wisdom and knowledge He has given me to make a decision already! He gave me a good brain; I should use it!

5. *Don't second-guess your decisions.* Once a decision has been made, unless you have a compelling reason, don't second-guess it! In my case, it would be don't fiftieth-guess it! It's entirely too easy for me to start questioning any decisions I make. I'm gifted in the second-guessing department. It reveals my lack of confidence in my ability to make good decisions. I tend to assume I'm going to make the wrong decision, and I can always look back on almost every decision I've made and conclude that it could have been better. That kind of thinking is so destructive! God didn't put me in this position to fail. He has equipped me with everything I need to do all that He has called me to do (Jeremiah 29:11–12; Philippians 1:6). God has equipped you to make good decisions for your family too!

> *If any of you lacks wisdom, he should ask God, who gives generously to all without finding fault, and it will be given to him. But when he asks, he must believe and not doubt, because he who doubts is like a wave of the sea, blown and tossed by the wind.*
>
> —JAMES 1:5–6

Sometimes others will second-guess your decisions for you. There will always be people in your life who will be more than happy to question your ability to do this single-parenting thing well. But if you have prayed, searched Scripture, spoken to others you trust, and researched the issues, you can confidently stand your ground in the face of opposition.

In my situation, my ex-husband sometimes doesn't agree with the decisions I make concerning our children. Our values and perspectives are different now. Thankfully, we've reached a point where we can disagree without angry words. The challenging thing is that I had always deferred to him on decision making. He had the final say at one time, but now I do. I know that he isn't praying about things or researching or seeking wise counsel, and that makes it very difficult to trust his opinion, although I do believe that God can still work through any broken vessel. But I believe that God is now going to lead my family through me, even though I'm most definitely a cracked pot myself!

SWEETNESS AND SORROW

There are innumerable instances when I feel acutely the lack of my children's father. I say it that way because in those moments it isn't so much that I miss my ex-husband as I miss the father of my children. There are times at games when I miss being able to turn to him and say, "Did you see that? Our son is amazing!" Or one of our children will do something hysterical, and I want to laugh with my ex-husband about how funny our children are. When we were married, even if he wasn't at certain events, I could still call him or share when he arrived home from work.

> *For this God is our God*
> *for ever and ever;*
> *he will be our guide*
> *even to the end.*
>
> —PSALM 48:14

I miss the man who was as emotionally invested in my children as I still am. No one else has quite the same interest in my children as their father did. I miss that. I miss having someone to share the burden of decision making. I miss having someone to figure out things with, such as which way to educate each child or how to navigate college financial aid. I miss having a fellow taxi driver to shuttle children to and from activities and school. I miss having a partner for all the everyday parenting adventures. I mourn my partner in marriage, but lately I mourn my partner in parenting even more.

Being a single parent at my children's events is often a very lonely thing. There are times when I feel as though I stick out like a sore thumb. I don't; I just feel that way. Most of the people at those events aren't even aware of my situation, but I'm acutely aware of it. I have to remind myself why I'm there. It isn't about me. I'm there to encourage, cheer for, and support my children. It's not a pity party for me. It's a celebration of them and their accomplishments. I try to be the best cheerleader I can be for my children, whether I'm standing on the sidelines alone or not.

When my ex-husband does attend events, we all sit together as a family—one great big dysfunctional family. It wasn't always that way. We used to sit across from each other and only nod at one another. Now we try to sit near each other. My ex-husband's wife doesn't attend my children's activities, so it isn't quite as awkward as it could be. But there are definitely times when it's a bit stressful to be sitting next to my married ex-husband. We aren't best friends anymore, and no matter how hard we try to act natural, there is a very unnatural aspect to the dynamics of our relationship.

Regardless of the unease, I believe my children really appreciate the effort we both make to attend their events. And each time we do sit or stand together, it gets easier to do it the next time. I'm thankful that God has enabled my ex-husband and me to support our children together. I pray that he will be able to attend more events. I think he is heading in that direction. My children need their dad to cheer from the sidelines, whether I want to stand next to him or not. I want them to know that they're more important than any relationship issues their father and I have—because they are.

Getting a Handle on Something Without a Handle

I will say, now that I'm further along in the single-parenting journey, people assume that I have it all together. That makes me chuckle. All together? Um, let's see. I could describe a typical week, day, or hour and dispel that notion in a heartbeat. I most definitely *don't* have a handle on this life. I'm not even touching the handle. Is there a handle?

For those of us who have been abandoned, the person who was supposed to be our biggest supporter and partner in all our parenting decisions has bailed on us. What do we do now? Here is what I *do* know, and this is really, really, really important, so take note: When people offer to help you, *take it*! Even if it's slightly inconvenient or embarrassing, let people bless you. With five children, I haven't found anything easy or uncomplicated about my life. But I had to stop worrying about people knowing I was in over my head and start learning to accept all the help I could get.

Now that I'm past the initial shock of adultery and divorce and into the everyday living of divorced single parenthood, I realize that it's my responsibility to share my needs with others. At the beginning of this tragedy, I didn't even have to ask for help; I just had to accept it. Now I need to step out of my comfort zone and ask. My friends are more than willing to help, but they all have their own stuff to deal with, so sometimes I just have to holler, "Help!"

Let me paint you a picture of life at my house. Last week was a nightmare of a week. Everything seemed to go wrong—two failed car inspections, one dental emergency, four dental appointments, three sick children, one doctor's appointment, one wet basement, two unexpected massive medical bills, one broken dishwasher, one faucet that won't stop spraying, two broken dresser drawers, one broken hallway shoe trunk, two missed deadlines, and one sinus infection. Throw on top of that the everyday stresses of single parenting, and it's all just a giant train wreck.

I finally texted a friend and asked if she could help me. She responded in seconds with a very happy "Yes!" I wish I had asked days before! I've finally learned to ask; now I need to learn not to wait until I'm in a state of emergency! A dear friend told me that I'm pretty much the poster child for needing assistance. I think she meant that in a positive way. (At least, I hope so.) We can all use a little help—or a lot of help—from time to time.

I want to encourage you to phone a friend! Please ask for and accept help. Being a single parent is very stressful. Allow people to alleviate some of the stress so that you can focus on what's really important. If you can get that house, car, and yard stuff dealt with, you can spend more time walking your sweet babes through this crazy life.

ALL I GOT . . . AND JESUS

When I began my single-mom journey, I had a vision for what I wanted the spiritual life of my family to look like. I felt certain I was going to be an awe-inspiring leader for my family. I'd always wanted my husband to pray with me and our children more, lead Bible-study time with our family, and take advantage of every teachable moment to point our family to the Lord.

I thought that now that it was all on me, I would step into that role and do it as I'd always wanted him to do it. What I found was that it was so much more difficult than I imagined. Working full-time, juggling the activities of my children, taking care of the house and finances, and dealing with all the different personalities in the family made it difficult for me to find the time to invest in family devotions or focused family prayer time, or even to take advantage of teachable moments.

My husband struggled with balancing all the demands on his time, and often, leading our family was put aside. Yes, I did want him to be more of a spiritual leader for us. Yes, I probably said it more times than I should have. I wanted the "perfect" scenario—daily prayer time, family devotions, and deep conversations at the dinner table. After he left, I soon found that finding the time and energy to pursue spiritual things in the way I would have liked was way tougher than I realized.

Here's what I've learned: Spiritual leadership really just requires a heart that's open to what God is doing in my family. By that I mean I might not be able to spend time preparing a devotional that will bless each of my children from teenager down to toddler, but I can share with them what God has been showing me lately while we're driving from activity to activity.

My oldest son and I discuss world events and how they relate to our faith. Those are some great conversations that help me think through my beliefs and convictions as they relate to real-world news. My oldest daughter and I share about relationships and treating others lovingly even when it's difficult to do so. She's at that age where friendship drama can be extreme at times. My middle son likes to get up early and do a devotional with me. When we can get ourselves out of bed, it's a very special time. He is also still my deep thinker, and we have many conversations about God, faith, and life issues. My youngest daughters like to read the Bible before bed and sing worship songs throughout the day. They are the easiest to guide spiritually, at least at this point!

Ultimately, my children just need me to love them well. I believe that raising them with a solid foundation of faith is imperative. That means that I spend time talking to them about the Lord, what He has done, what He is doing, and how His Word applies to our lives. It means that I invest time and thought into strengthening their faith by how I live, what I say, and what we talk about. Although I know what it means to teach my children spiritual truths, it's difficult to know how to do that in a practical way every day.

I think most of us don't have a firm idea of what being a spiritual leader for our family really looks like. It's something to strive for, but in this crazy life we live, it seems impossible at times.

I've found that leading at home is full of distractions. So many things grab my attention—chores, bills, homework, making dinner . . . you know the drill. It feels as if there are at least fifty-seven activities a day that pull my family away from the things I'd like for us to do. My sister recently encouraged me when I was lamenting how difficult it was to lead spiritually. She said, "You lead your family by the way you are and how you live." That was such a comfort.

I think the biggest lesson I've learned is that this single-parenting life isn't about me doing something, or anything, perfectly. It isn't about how well I lead, organize, train, or discipline. I don't believe this is about me *doing*; it's about me *being*—being available for God to lead and use. My prayers are no longer only that I can be a better mom, that I can handle the stress better, or that I can get it all together. My prayers are now primarily that God would love my children through me. I pray that they would know that He is enough and that He can work mighty and wonderful things in their lives, hearts, and minds not because I do such a great job but because He is such a great God.

I wish I were better suited for single parenthood, but the reality is, I wasn't made to be both Momma and Daddy. Neither were you. I wish I had more to give to my children than my exhausted, overwhelmed, emotional, single-mommy self—but this is all I got. All I got . . . and Jesus. And when I consider Him, that's a lot!

Father, this single-parenting thing is so difficult. It's nearly impossible to do it well. Lord, You say that You will give us all we need to do all that You have called us to do (Philippians 4:19). Enable us, please. We want so desperately to love our children well. Please pour Your love all over them, using us as Your vessels. Give us wisdom and discernment as parents. Lord, please show us special ways we can bless each of our children as individuals—ways we can encourage them, love on them, and teach them about You. Father, forgive us for our fear, our frustration, and our failings as parents. Please change our hearts to reflect Yours.

Oh, Father, be the perfect Father our children need so desperately. May they find their true identity in Christ. May they grow to be men and women who know who they are in Christ. We ask that they, as God's holy and beloved children, will have compassionate hearts; will treat others with "kindness, humility, gentleness and patience"; and will be forgiving, loving, and thankful people (Colossians 3:12–15). Lord, show us how to be the parents You have called us to be.

In Jesus' name, amen.

TEN

I'd Dream, but That Would Require Sleeping

"For I know the plans I have for you," declares the LORD, *"plans for wholeness and not for evil, to give you a future and a hope. Then you will call upon me and come and pray to me, and I will hear you. You will seek me and find me. When you seek me with all your heart, I will be found by you," declares the* LORD.

—JEREMIAH 29:11–14, ESV

This chapter could also be called the "I want" chapter.

Well, I guess you can probably figure out that my vocational dream is writing. I'd love to write books that inspire and Bible studies that challenge and bless. I think there isn't a more perfect job in the whole wide world—my face buried in Scripture, praying for the Holy Spirit to reveal great truths, and then the added blessing of being able to share it all with others. I get goose bumps just thinking about it.

I have other dreams, too.

I want my children to know the Lord. I guess I should clarify: I want them not to just know who the Lord is but to really truly know the Lord. I want my children to know Him so well that they can't help but be passionate disciples. I want them to know intimately the love of their Savior. I want them to never doubt His love, His sovereignty, or His purpose for their lives. I want them to trust Him wholeheartedly.

I want my children to live wonderful lives free from pain and suffering. I know that's a dream because, if nothing else, I've learned that this life will never be free of pain and suffering. Proverbs 19:23, one of my favorite verses, says, "The fear of the LORD leads to life: Then one rests content, untouched by trouble." I don't believe this means that we are immune from distress and disaster because we fear God. My life is a testament to the fact that no one is immune from trouble. What I believe it means is that we are untouched by trouble at our core. Trouble cannot destroy us when we belong to the Lord.

Journal entry: Lord, I don't know what to do. I don't know what to think or say or pray. I'm lost in my thoughts. There are too many voices in my head. Lord, please sift through it all and make it clear what I am to think and believe and hope for. Lord, I think one of the loudest voices is the one that says that I'm going to be alone forever, that You are going to teach me lesson upon lesson about You being my everything, and I'll have to learn to live alone. Is that from You, Lord? Do You desire me to be alone? You have put such a desire in me to be a wife and helpmate. I loved being married.

If I get to do it again, Lord, I want to be a godly woman who brings strength to the marriage instead of someone who loses herself in it. I want to be a whole woman. Lord, maybe I still need to find myself, my calling, my dreams, my direction . . . What do You want, Lord? Lord, could You please direct me very clearly? And where I'm missing Your leading, could You slap me upside the head so I'm aware of Your plan and what steps I should take?

I'm realizing that Jesus is enough. I haven't learned it, fully compre-
hended it, or understood it completely yet, but I know that He is enough.
I want my children to know, as I do, that if we let Him, He will fill the
deep, dark, desperate places of our hearts and make us whole. He is the
Healer of our souls, the Keeper of our hearts, and the Love of our lives.
We must turn to Him before we turn to anyone else. God will bring us to
difficult places, but He will also bring us through them.

Sometimes I might be weary, exhausted, angry, sorrowful, and frustrated, but I know that at the end of the day, God is faithful, merciful, and
loving. I know that I can trust Him. I give all those hurt feelings to Him.
I tell Him about them. I ask for help dealing with them, and I believe He
will. I have confidence because I have a great Savior. I need a great Savior.

I want my children to be fortified against the temptations that have
plagued my ex-husband's family for years. I want my children to be
strengthened against the things I struggle with—and there are so many.
I want my children to know to their core that their strength comes from
the Lord—not me, not them, not church. It only comes from Jesus!

BIG, LOVELY DREAMS

I want to find love again. I'm just being totally honest. I loved being a
wife. I miss it desperately at times. I miss my companion, my friend, and
my lover. I miss the interaction—the fun banter, the serious conversations, even the fights. I miss thinking about what I can do to make my
husband happy. I know that sounds old-fashioned, but I really liked making myself pretty for him, preparing things for him, and even thinking of
little ways to make life easier for him.

My ex-husband had a tendency to step on odd things and get hurt. It
didn't matter if the hallway was clear (which it rarely was); he would always find the one thing that hurt—the needle in the carpet as it were. He

usually came home late, so after the kids were in bed, I'd make sure the path was clear wherever I thought he would be walking. It sounds silly now, but I loved being his helpmate. I miss it more than I can say. I don't know if God's plan includes another husband in my future. I hope it does.

It's funny that I'm writing about this now, because recently my five-year-old asked me all kinds of questions about her daddy and why he didn't live with us anymore. She asked if I loved him. I told her that I loved him very much when we got married and that I didn't want him to leave. She asked if her daddy loved me. I said that he loved someone else now. Then I realized I shouldn't have said that—I don't want to lie to her, but I also don't want her to think that love is just something that comes and goes based on how we feel. I believe that love is a choice, and it's hard work.

She said she wants a daddy who lives with us. I told her we can pray for God to give us a godly, loving man to live with us and be my husband and her daddy. She was happy with that thought, but I had to say that God might have something else in store for us. We don't know what God's perfect plan is; we just have to trust Him. She and I are hoping and praying, though.

I believe it is important that we are cautious and prayerful as we deal with our loneliness. I mentioned earlier that after my husband left, I struggled with the temptation of wanting a relationship. The year after my divorce, I became friends with another single parent—a man who had experienced similar circumstances. We got our kids together often and had many conversations about the challenges of single parenting and divorce that we were dealing with on a daily basis. At some point along the way, I changed from enjoying the friendship to hoping for more.

Although he didn't ask for it, I found myself taking on more of a helpmate role than a friendship role with him. I found myself happily doing things for him like providing childcare, planning meals, helping with transportation, planning birthday parties and holiday celebrations, and going on shopping trips. That list is honestly a bit embarrassing, but that was me—running myself ragged for my family and his. I was a crazy woman.

I was trying to "fix" my solitary situation in my own way and in my own timing. My focus was on filling an empty spot. I was lonely and I didn't enjoy doing this life without my partner, my husband. My quest for companionship wasn't healthy. I needed to be in a much better place.

Then one night God got my attention. I was reading a Bible story to my children about when the Israelites demanded a human king. God told them that He was all they needed, that no one would or could take care of them as well as He. But the Israelites insisted. They wanted a king they could see. So God gave them King Saul.

Saul started out great, but he soon deteriorated into a proud, arrogant, and disobedient king. God gave the people what they wanted, and it ended up being a seriously bad thing for them.

At that moment, I realized that I was just like the Israelites, who wanted a flesh-and-blood king. I wanted a husband I could see and touch, but God had already assured me that He was my Husband. He could and would be all that I needed. Unfortunately, although I understood the application of the story to my life, my emotions took a bit of time catching up with my brain. It was ridiculous how I could convince myself that whatever I wanted could be good for me. Fortunately, God pursued me and finally got my attention through circumstances, conversations with friends, and a big dose of reality.

I eventually recognized that although I would love to have a husband, I wanted God's best for me at the right time. This is definitely the right place for me to be—not desperate to fill a void but desperate to be where God wants me.

I think most of us know that if we are content with our lives, we are in the best place for God to bring someone special to share our lives with. I've said, "I want to be a whole person before I get into a relationship again." Whole person. What do I mean by that? I believe that means that I'm not dependent on another person to ensure my happiness. I might want to be in a relationship, and I might hope and pray for one, but I understand that God will provide me with everything I need to find peace and joy even if He calls me to be single. I do hope to be married again someday. If I'm blessed with another husband, I hope and pray that I will come to the relationship recognizing that my completeness is in Christ and all that I need comes from Him.

Although I would love to remarry, my dreams are so much more than that. I'm hoping to be a writer who inspires, encourages, and blesses others. I really hope that God will use this dreadful experience in my life for good. I know that He will. Actually, He already has.

I have other dreams—some silly, some serious. I want to be a joyful half-marathon runner, not just a fast-moving complainer. I'd love to live in a beautiful house at the beach or a lovely, old, renovated rural farmhouse; take some international missions trips; sing with a full orchestra; and learn to knit, crochet, shoot a gun, and maybe even engage in some hand-to-hand combat. And, no, the last two dreams aren't directed at anyone in particular!

This is what I want you to do, my friend: When you have a minute (probably at two o'clock in the morning), I want you to make three lists. For the first list, write down your hopes and dreams for yourself; then make another list of your hopes and dreams for your children. And if, like me, you would like to remarry someday, make a third list of those qualities you hope for in a future spouse. I call that list my knight-in-shining-armor list.

My first qualification is that my hoped-for partner be passionate about the Lord—seriously passionate. And, friend, don't you dare compromise on the most important qualities on your list just because you're lonely. If your potential spouse meets all 24,999 things on your list but isn't passionate about the Lord, he or she isn't worth it. And, really—I mean *really*—Jesus is our true Knight in shining armor. So for now I'm having my coffee dates with Jesus. I've decided it's most important that I fall in love with Him before I fall in love with anyone else.

Being single is certainly not on my list of dreams, but being where God wants me will always be the biggest thing on my list. I don't know where God will have me in five or ten years. Actually, five or ten weeks is a mystery as well. I used to hate it when someone would say something about the fact that maybe God wants me to remain single until the end of my life. I absolutely didn't want to hear it. But I have to be real and say it also annoys me if people predict that I will remarry someday.

Honestly, I simply don't know what God has planned for me. I would never have predicted adultery, divorce, and single parenthood being my reality. Now, I'm okay with being single indefinitely—not thrilled but okay. I know that God is enough. I know that Jesus loves me better than anyone else ever could. That doesn't stop me from dreaming, praying, and hoping, but it's all covered with a great big trust that God knows what is absolutely best for me.

I can't help but wonder where God will have me in the future. He might have a wonderful plan that involves teaching children on the mission field. I might get to write Bible studies and more books. And I might just get to be blessed as I continue reading other people's books and studying other writers' Bible studies. My goal is to live my life to His glory wherever He puts me. He has a best plan for your life, too. And He has already put it into motion!

I don't know what dreams you have, but dream big! We have a big God who loves to be kind to us. I believe that God made us to dream big dreams. We know that all of our dreams don't come true—we have lived that reality—but we also know that God can do great things despite our circumstances.

The Best Perspective

A few years back, my small group from church did an intriguing study on heaven. Pondering heaven definitely made me more interested in getting there. I had always viewed heaven as my dream vacation. Now, I can say that my life circumstances have made me long for it even more. I'm blessed as a Christian to not just hope I'm going to get there but to know that someday it's going to be reality. And I simply can't wait. Every time the sky is beautiful, I say, "Those look like great clouds for Jesus to come through, don't you think?" My kids are probably getting tired of me saying it, but I'm waiting with great anticipation. I haven't always been that way, but I believe that Jesus wants us all to look forward to heaven.

This world is a tiresome place to live in. I long for my perfect home, the beautiful house in heaven that Jesus is even now preparing for me (John 14:1–3). There will be no more dusty shelves, sticky counters, or messy rooms. No more heartbreak or bad experiences. No more worries, aches, pains, or tears. I can't wait!

My children and I talk about heaven a lot. We share the questions we'll ask the Lord, and the things we'd like to tell Him. I probably joke too much. I tell them that Jesus is going to greet me with a large, greasy pepperoni pizza—I'm fairly certain I will be able to eat cheese in heaven. One of my sons asked me if we would sleep in heaven. I said that right now that sounded heavenly, but I thought we wouldn't need it there. But I'm still counting on a hammock with a view! I don't mean to be silly; I just find such joy in imagining what heaven will be like. It might be totally different from my mind's portrayal, but I know that God takes pleasure in my dreams of heaven. Thinking about what lies ahead gives me a greater expectation and keeps my focus on the things of the Lord rather than on the things of this world.

The future that God has planned for us—both our earthly and heavenly futures—is beyond our imaginings, I'm sure. I know that my eternal future will more than make up for my present circumstances and difficulties. This will all be worth it in the end.

So dream a big dream for your time on earth, and dream an even bigger dream for eternity to come! And please remember that God thinks you are simply wonderful, and He has a beautiful plan for your life. You need not fear or worry; He's got you covered.

Father, we are going to dream big dreams, trusting that You have big plans for our lives. Your Word says that Your plans for us are good and perfect (Jeremiah 29:11; Romans 12:2). Lord, please give us grace to wait with expectation and faith, trusting that the circumstances You've allowed in our lives are preparing us for a better future than we could ever imagine (Psalm 27:14; Psalm 130:5–6; Isaiah 30:18). Thank You for the promise of heaven—for our eternal inheritance that is "imperishable, undefiled, and unfading, kept in heaven" for us (1 Peter 1:3–4, ESV). And not only are You keeping our inheritance for us; You are perfectly keeping us—guarding us through faith (1 Peter 1:5). Lord, we are so thankful for the hope of things to come.

In Jesus' name, amen.

ELEVEN

The Man Chapter: Same Pain, Different Perspective

You keep him in perfect peace whose mind is stayed on you,
because he trusts in you. Trust in the LORD forever, for the
LORD God is an everlasting rock.

—ISAIAH 26:3–4, ESV

I've written this book from the viewpoint of an abandoned wife, but the fact is that there are abandoned husbands, too, and if you're in that category, I want to offer you hope as well. To be perfectly honest, this has been a difficult chapter for me to write. While there are absolutely things we all feel—universal themes that ring true regardless of gender—I know that men and women react to and process experiences differently.

I've spoken with men who have suffered abandonment and I've been privileged to walk with friends through their pain. Still, although I've had many conversations and asked many questions, I must admit that I'm very aware that I may never be able to fully understand a man's heart or mind. But I will share what they have shared with me. And I pray that together we will see that God works in the lives of both men and women whose hearts have been broken and lives have been altered by the destructive actions of their spouses.

That initial emotional punch to the gut hits with the same ferocity whether the receiver is male or female. I kept looking for the big differ-ence—the giant glaringly obvious disparity. Surely we must feel things differently. But what I have found is that we are surprisingly the same in our heartbreak. We feel pain exactly the same, and yet it's no surprise that we are quite different in our reactions and perspective. We've each lost something we valued beyond measure, something we felt confident was ours for a lifetime.

We feel duped, bewildered, and incapable of fixing the most im-portant relationship in our lives. Our questions are constant: How did I not see this coming? How could this person who loved me so much hurt me so dramatically and permanently? How did things change so drastically? None of our questions will have answers sufficient to allevi-ate our pain.

It seems to some degree that no matter how many issues we had or didn't have in our marriages, we all feel ambushed by abandonment, be-wildered by the betrayal. The gut-wrenching pain is so much more than an emotional experience. It's excruciating. It's physical, mental, and spiri-tual. Others may think they understand the pain, but no one can truly comprehend the depth of it. It shakes us to our core. Who we are emo-tionally, mentally, physically, and spiritually is all called into question.

And for a moment, all seems lost; *we* seem lost. But we're not.

This situation forces us to redefine ourselves in ways we had never imagined. That redefining process doesn't change our identity in Christ. We must remind ourselves of who we are in Him. One gentleman told me, "Even though a difficult situation has happened in my life, I still hope and trust in Jesus. I don't understand it fully, but I trust in His unfailing love for me." No sin, whether ours or someone else's, can separate us from the love of God. We are loved more than we can comprehend. We are strengthened beyond our understanding. No failure is too great for God to use for good.

After living your life as a married man and father, how do you now define yourself in your newly altered circumstances? You're now divorced and maybe even a single dad. I know that pain. No matter how common divorce is today, it seems we all feel as if we carry around the scarlet letter *D* on our backs, on our chests, on our foreheads, everywhere. It is unavoidable and painful. The simplest task of filling out a form for school or a doctor's appointment is torturous the first time we check the "divorced" box. We now own that box. Unfortunately it's ours, but it doesn't make us lesser people. It's our marital status, not our defining feature. The question is, how do we move forward strengthened, resolved, and empowered to honor God with our inward and outward lives?

The natural inclination of men is to work harder when faced with difficulties—to find the solution to the problem, implement it, and move on. You have probably found that this situation presents problems with no easy solutions. You cannot start with simply fixing the problem. You must start with a solid recognition of who you are in Christ. It isn't about what you do or how well you do it. It isn't about success or performance or ability. Your identity is found neither in the things you accomplish nor in the failures you endure. It's found in the person of Jesus and His righteousness.

God made us all with a need for affirmation and respect, which was to be fulfilled through a relationship with Him. We have turned this need on its ear and made it about our own work, accomplishments, and righteousness rather than about Jesus' work and accomplishment on the cross and His imputed righteousness. The irony of our struggle is that there really should be no struggle. Christ has accomplished it all to provide everything we were made to need.

I have spent hours and hours searching for the "answer" to the question, "What does a man replace his drive for success, accomplishment, and affirmation with after a divorce?" I realized it isn't about a man re-placing his drive—that's a God-given drive. It's about changing a para-digm, exchanging his way of thinking for God's way of thinking.

I'm reminded of Micah 6:8: "He has told you, O man, what is good; and what does the LORD require of you but to do justice, and to love kindness, and to walk humbly with your God?" (ESV). Humility. I'd say we got a good dose of humility in our divorces, but that isn't the kind of humility God requires of us. It's the chosen humility of deciding that our lives, our goals, our motivations are less important than His. He is trust-worthy. We can trust Him with our lives. He is good. He will take all we entrust to Him and care for it exceedingly well.

DIFFERENT PERCEPTIONS OF THE SAME PAIN

Sharing what women and men have in common is quite easy. Sharing what we don't, not so much. There are obvious differences—some that stick out like sore thumbs. I believe that we women tend to struggle with our core identity in response to adultery. We constantly ask, "What is wrong with me that my husband would leave?" It's more a reflection of who we are as women rather than how we fulfilled our roles as wives.

Men, on the other hand, seem to view their spouses' abandonment as a reflection of the job they did as husbands. They tend to say things like, "I could have done better."

A woman usually focuses on relationships, and a man focuses on goals. How does that play out in this scenario? I believe women want to improve themselves, whereas men want to improve the way they do things. I'm tempted to say that it's personal for a woman and perfor-mance for a man.

I believe that it is personal for both of us at the start, but as we process it and move forward, our perspectives diverge. A woman focuses on herself as a person. A man focuses on himself as a performer. And neither is wrong. It's how God wired us. Those differences are His design to bless us and enable us to complement each other in our marriages. Unfortunately, in our circumstances, those gender differences become the tools for picking up the pieces after divorce rather than the qualities we use to complement our spouses.

I once heard someone say, "I don't like the way emotions make me feel." Amen to that. Women are, by nature, more emotional and intuitive. We approach tragedy feeling way more than any person should be expected to feel. We process all our decisions, actions, and reactions through our broken hearts—with an emphasis on the word *broken*. During and after my divorce, I often commented that I shouldn't be allowed to make decisions based on anything but pure facts until my heart healed. How can anyone trust a broken heart?

I believe that men process all these things so differently. You are logical in your summation of the situation and can approach it that way. To some degree, you have the ability to look at it objectively with the idea of just moving forward and focusing on the new job before you. Most of the men I interviewed used phrases similar to "just do it" to describe their attitude about life. You're able to look at things without your personal feelings being the overriding factor in your decisions. Facts over feelings. (I so wish I could live that way, at least part of the time.)

While researching gender differences in dealing with divorce, I was reminded of the story of David and Bathsheba and the death of their newborn son. While the child was alive, David fasted, prayed, and lay on the floor, ignoring all those who implored him to rise. When the child died, David's servants feared informing him because they thought he might harm himself. But to their surprise, when he suspected that his son had died, he rose, washed, anointed himself, changed clothes, and went into the house of the Lord to worship.

His servants felt compelled to ask why David's behavior changed so suddenly at the news of his son's death. David responded,

> While the child was still alive, I fasted and wept, for I said, "Who knows whether the LORD will be gracious to me, that the child may live?" But now he is dead. Why should I fast? Can I bring him back again? I shall go to him, but he will not return to me. (2 Samuel 12:22–23, ESV)

I thought how differently I would have responded—definitely more weeping and mourning for days on end. David's response was very much like a typical man—and I mean that in a good way. Praise God that he gave men the ability to move forward, to lead through battles and difficulties, to face trials without the paralysis of emotions run amuck. David's goal in his fasting, praying, and weeping was the healing of his son. When God's answer was a definite no, David moved forward in that new knowledge.

That seemed to be a common response of the men I interviewed. Once they had fought valiantly for their marriages but lost, they decided it was time to move forward. New marching orders had been received.

G's journal entry: I knew there was no going back at this point in our relationship, and I had to man up and get on with it. All the while knowing that I was in good hands and trusting in God as my solid foundation. . . . All that said . . . I still had lost my friend, whom I had spent most of my life with.

Failure Is a Pain

A difficulty I see men experiencing is the perception of failure that often accompanies the loss of their marriage. It's easy to see divorce as failure, whether we view it as personal or performance based. Some of the men I spoke with tended to share that they felt they had failed to take care of things well. They had failed their children by not doing whatever would have averted this disaster. They had failed to set their priorities properly. I guess my response is, who of us hasn't failed at one time or another?

Unfortunately, we have a definite inability to be perfect. No matter what our actual or perceived failures may have been, our marriages were sacred ground. They were covenants that were to be upheld and fought for to the death. Unbelievably, our spouses chose to fight against those covenants.

Notice that I referred to "perceived failures" in the previous paragraph. After hearing the stories of several men, I would say that often their perception of their role in the abandonment of their spouses was, in my opinion, too harsh. Granted, I come from a place of extreme identification with abandoned spouses, but I believe there is simply no excuse for anyone committing adultery or abandoning his or her marriage. No matter how lousy a spouse we were or how unhappy our spouse was, that doesn't give our spouse the right to opt out of the covenant.

As Christians, we have the power and strength of God to fulfill the roles He has given us. Not all our callings are easy. I believe He desires us to be happy in our marriages, to see marriage as a beautiful picture of His relationship with us. I also believe that God made marriage for the primary purpose of making us holy, not necessarily happy. It's a lot easier to deal with challenging issues when we know that God is fulfilling His purpose in our lives through them.

To me, marriage was truly for better or worse. I remember my first argument with my husband. It was a minor incident, but I was sure upset, and I wanted to get away from him, badly. I distinctly remember realizing that I couldn't just walk out the door. I was stuck there with him, and at that moment, it wasn't a terribly comforting thought. But that realization was foundational to my marriage. I guess I just never imagined divorce as an option, so leaving my marriage was out of the question.

And yet, seventeen years later I found myself filing for divorce after being abandoned by my husband, with no hope of reconciliation. I never would have thought I'd admit defeat in my marriage. I'm sure many of us in this kind of situation feel that way.

Trading the Pain of Our Self-image for the Power of a Christ-Image

Questioning ourselves and our actions before, during, and after our divorce produces the same need for affirmation in both men and women. We all want to survive this ordeal and be okay, maybe even respected and loved. It's an upward battle to just feel "normal" again. The reality is that this life—this divorced, difficult existence—is our new normal. I seriously hate that phrase *new normal*. It implies that on some level, I consider this divorced, single-parent life to be normal. I don't. It's not right and never will be. Unfortunately, it's where I am, and it's where you are, too.

How do we get the affirmation we need so desperately? As a woman, I get affirmation from my relationships with others. I want to know someone thinks I'm beautiful, inside and out. I want to feel cherished, loved, and valued as a woman. As a man, you get affirmation from what you accomplish and produce, the roles you fill. You want to feel respected and valued as a man. I'll tell you one thing: No one is going to be able to affirm us as well as the Lord. It's that simple . . . and that complicated.

Many of the men I spoke with honestly shared that their initial search for affirmation came through relationships with women rather than the Lord. I understand that. I suspect that's the case for many of us. We find comfort in the arms of another person rather than in the Lord. That's why I said that looking to the Lord for our affirmation is both simple and complicated. It's so easy to reach for the nearest human being who is willing to look into our eyes, speak the words we want to hear, and make us feel the way we want to feel, even if it's all fleeting. Short-term gain—effective but not lasting. Ultimately, it only adds to our pain and emptiness.

The whole finding-our-identity-in-Jesus thing takes effort, focus, and determination. It takes setting aside our natural inclination to seek comfort from another person or our countless activities. It takes releasing our hold on our natural tendencies so that our grip can be firmly fixed on Christ. It's reading and applying God's Word and prioritizing Him in our lives.

When you have a spare minute (because that's usually all we have), how do you spend it? Where do you put your effort? It may be easy to focus on work, your kids, your hobbies, your health, and your house, but it's extremely challenging to turn that focus on the Lord. Take that goal-oriented, focused drive to accomplish great things and turn it to your relationship with the Lord. The benefits far outweigh any inconvenience. I know it's challenging, but it's worth it.

When seeking the Lord, you may not find the instant gratification you normally feel when you accomplish a task, reach a goal, or fulfill a need. Pursuing a relationship with the Lord doesn't necessarily feel as though you've performed any great thing. But you have. You've fulfilled a vital need in your own life by allowing God to use you to love, guide, and fight for those He has placed in your life. You are fulfilling a noble goal of being an honorable, wise, and loving man.

You have accomplished the task of gaining wisdom and knowledge by immersing yourself in God's Word. Pursuing a relationship with the Lord is an intentional goal for each day, not just for your life. In knowing Him, you not only find peace that passes all understanding, but you gain His wisdom and strength for the challenges you face in life (Philippians 4:6–7; Psalm 111:10; 2 Samuel 22:33, 40)! Grab hold of Him and be empowered!

Proverbs 14:26 says, "In the fear of the LORD one has strong confidence, and his children will have a refuge" (ESV). Your relationship with the Lord is imperative not only for you as a man, but also for you as a father. Your children need to see your perspective coming from God's Word and your hope, strength, and peace coming from your Savior. Your source of strength, and theirs, is the Lord (2 Chronicles 16:9; Habakkuk 3:19). What a valuable life-affirming lesson to impart to your children!

I'm still learning how to balance all my roles, and unfortunately, the spiritual-leadership role often gets placed at the bottom of the list. It should be the most important thing I do. I do believe that God enables us to do all the things He has called us to do. We are uniquely equipped for our calling, no matter how challenging it is. Our role, our most important role, is to train our children well, to raise them to love the Lord with all their hearts, souls, minds, and strength (Mark 12:30). God has equipped us for this role; now we need to just do it (Ephesians 1:3)!

Yet we cannot fulfill that role with any success if we aren't training ourselves as well. We need to approach our spiritual lives with the same

J's journal entry: I have an unwavering, tireless commitment to do what is right. I still believe in commitment. Whenever I feel like giving up, I'll still do what's right. And I'll teach this lesson to my children.

tenacity, focus, and strength with which we approach all our other responsibilities. This is warfare. We must be willing to lay everything down for the Lord and fight with abandon for our lives and the lives of our children.

We can't assume that teaching our children about the Lord will come naturally, without any intentional effort on our part. We would never think of allowing our children to go hungry, thirsty, unclothed, or uneducated. We'd never consider taking blessings away from them simply because those blessings were inconveniences to us. So why do we sometimes leave by the wayside the most important knowledge we can give them: that God deeply loves and esteems them, that He has a wonderful plan for their lives, and that their identity isn't in their own abilities or accomplishments, but in Christ?

It isn't that we don't want to share that knowledge with our children—and even ourselves. I believe most of us absolutely do want that. It's just that we live in triage mode most of the time. Whatever is bleeding the most gets the most attention. Unfortunately, nothing can really be dropped—it's all important and maybe even good. And yet the best thing—the true source of strength, peace, and wisdom that is ours for the taking and giving, that is ours if we would just accept it—is often laid aside.

GIVING OUR PAIN TO THE ONE WHO CAN HANDLE IT

Why is it so difficult to turn to the Lord, to find our identity, purpose, and strength in Him? I still struggle at times with feeling like I can handle it all—"Thanks, God, but I got this." The majority of men I spoke with shared that they tried most often to handle things alone.

One gentleman said, "I probably tried to do most of it alone until it was in the too-hard-to-do box." He said that he was always concerned about being a burden to others. It's difficult to share our tragedy with others. It's too easy to feel judged and to assume we'll be labeled as failures. We aren't failures! Our marriages may have failed, but we aren't defined by that reality. Our lives always have more value than we think they do.

You are so much more than a divorcé; you are a man God designed for great things. Your life has meaning far beyond what you can imagine. This annoying divorced state is unavoidably a significant feature of your life now. It's something that has changed the direction of your life, but you must not let it define you, lest you become an angry, bitter person. Define yourself by who you are in Christ. Let God take this change and do with it as He will.

With God, these unwanted, life-altering circumstances can still become positive experiences in our lives. He can make even the most tragic situation into something that brings us good. It seems trite to write that phrase. This tragedy can bring us good? Seriously?

Yet I can attest to the inconceivable ability of God to take a painful place in my life and turn it into a beautiful place of healing. I believe that

> W's journal entry: I used to find my identity in what I did. . . . "I do a great job . . . Look at my beautiful wife . . . Look at my great kids." I can't seek my identity there anymore. It's not about my success, performance, or righteousness. It's about Jesus' righteousness. Society wants to push me in the direction of "all about me." It wants me to compensate for my mistakes. I don't have that need anymore. Jesus has made up for my mistakes. God has got my back. Focusing on God takes away my agenda.

I'm a stronger individual—more focused, more understanding, more merciful, more loving—than I ever was before. I have a hyperfocused perspective on life now. I know what I want to get out of it and put into it.

It has been a painful process that I don't ever want to relive, but I'm thankful for the results. I've grown as a woman. I want to be this person I am becoming. I like her better. I'm still a mess—scatterbrained, slightly more prone to tears over both happy and sad things, less task oriented, and more people oriented—but I'm a happy mess.

I'm also less needy than I used to be, even though my needs are far greater than they've ever been. I've often said that God is using these challenging circumstances to make me into the person He has always wanted me to be. I'm much better as a healed person than I ever was as someone who was simply well.

Are you becoming a man you like through this process? Someone you can be proud of? Do you see God changing your heart in ways you never imagined? Do you sense God leading you in new ways? If you don't yet, pray that God will give you His perspective, and that you will sense His leading and catch a glimpse of His plan for you. He has a plan, and it's good. I promise!

Father, You are intimately acquainted with betrayal and yet continue to respond in love (Luke 23:34). That seems nearly impossible for us. Lord, we are wounded and bleeding, and we need Your healing, Your strength, and Your assurance that we have not lost everything (Psalm 147:3). Lord, please help us to find our affirmation in You and You alone (2 Corinthians 1:21–22). We know that You love us deeply not because of anything we have or have not done (Romans 5:6–8). Your love for us is complete, unending, and unconditional (Psalm 100:5; Ephesians 3:14–19). We want to find our identity in You, Lord, but it is so challenging when everything else cries out for our attention and focus. It is so easy to feel validated by our jobs or roles in the community and church, but, Father, we know You are where our strength lies (2 Samuel 22:40; Psalm 73:26; Isaiah 40:31). Lord, we feel compelled to fix this situation, but it is clear we cannot fix it. Everything is under Your control, not ours (Matthew 19:26). Father, help us to trust You more. Please help us make the time to be in fellowship with You. Father, we ask that You make us into spiritual leaders who lead bravely, pray diligently, and love well (Ephesians 4:1–3; 1 Thessalonians 5:16–18).

In Your Son's name we pray, amen.

TWELVE

The New Me

*The LORD is near to the brokenhearted and saves the crushed
in spirit. Many are the afflictions of the righteous, but the
LORD delivers him out of them all.*

—PSALM 34:18–19, ESV

As I walked through the first year of my family's tragedy, I found myself
in the story of the Israelites. I don't mean that I found myself reading
their story a lot. I mean that I identified very much with the Israelites
and their plight. I knew suffering and could see how God was rescuing,
providing for, and protecting my family.

The story of the Israelites at the Red Sea has particularly blessed me.
The Israelites had just been released from captivity and were heading
away from Egypt. When they reached the Red Sea, with mountains on
either side of them, they looked back and saw the Egyptian army fast
approaching. It must have seemed like a hopeless situation. I'm sure, just
like the Israelites, I would have been questioning God's plan when that
scenario unfolded.

As I watched my family fall apart, I often found myself wondering
about God's good and perfect plan. I understood those poor, hurting,
terrified Israelites. The beauty of that story is that God was making a way
through their crisis before they even knew they needed it.

During the first summer of our family tragedy, a guest preacher spoke
at church about the wind that parted the water to provide an escape route

for the Israelites. Exodus 14:21 says that "the LORD drove the sea back with a strong east wind," which implies that the wind came from the other shoreline toward them. Do you see the glorious wonder in that? God parted the water toward them, not away from them. He was making the path for their escape before they could see it. He brought it to them!

I was so excited when I heard this. After church I said to my kids, "Did you hear that? God is making a way for us even now! We just don't know what it's going to look like. I bet it will be better than anything we can imagine!" There is so much to that Red Sea story. I love what God said to Israel through Moses. While the Israelites were freaking out—which was a standard response for them (and me)—God told them,

> Fear not, stand firm, and see the salvation of the LORD, which he
> will work for you today. For the Egyptians whom you see today, you
> shall never see again. The LORD will fight for you, and you have only
> to be silent. (Exodus 14:13–14, ESV)

If that isn't a word for me, I'm not sure what is. Hush. Be still. Watch what God is going to do. I try hard to be quiet, still, and watchful. And sometimes I even succeed.

In *My Utmost for His Highest*, Oswald Chambers wrote a devotional that touched my heart:

> If we believe in Jesus, it is not what we gain, but what He pours
> through us that counts. It is not that God makes us beautifully
> rounded grapes, but that He squeezes the sweetness out of us.
> Spiritually, we cannot measure our life by success, but only by what
> God pours through us, and we cannot measure that at all. . . . "He
> that believeth in me out of him shall flow rivers of living water"—
> hundreds of other lives will be continually refreshed. It is time now

to break the life, to cease craving for satisfaction, and to spill the thing out.*

I love the visual of round, plump grapes being squeezed so that the lovely, sweet juice flows out. I pray that my life would be marked by the sweetness of Christ spilling from my thoughts, actions, and words. I'm afraid that sometimes the only thing spilling from me is self. I know that God has good intentions for me; I just wish that He defined *good* the same way I do.

Here's my definition: *Good* means no pain, no sorrow, no betrayal, no sacrifices; everyone does what I ask when I ask it; I have time for everything I want to do; people love me; I get to do whatever I want; nobody says "stupid" or "shut up"; my kids get along perfectly; I'm happily married; I'm madly in love with my husband, and more importantly, he's madly in love with me. Although I think God would say most of those things are good, I don't believe that those things are measures of the good He wants to do in my life.

His definition would probably be more like this: *Good* is whatever draws you closer to Me and makes you more like Me; it allows you to experience the beauty of trusting Me and shows you that I love you too much to just make you happy, because I long to make you holy.

It's difficult after a personal tragedy to get to a place where you think, *God, I trust You completely, and I know that You will get me through anything, even if it's another nightmare!* Not so easy to say either.

I spent many months waiting for the next disaster to strike. I know that sounds a bit silly, but because something horrible happened to me, it was way too easy to think that God was just going to keep pounding me until I got whatever He wanted me to get. I finally realized that this

---

* Oswald Chambers, *My Utmost for His Highest* (New Jersey: Barbour, 1963), 181.

wasn't God's way. God uses our difficulties to refine us—to strengthen us and ultimately to bless us, not to punish or browbeat us.

People would remind me that I should "count it all joy" to suffer, that suffering is sharing in an experience with Christ and is truly a gift (James 1:2–4, ESV). I always wanted to respond, "Did you seriously just say that out loud to me?" (Word of advice: Don't say this to someone going through a divorce!)

> *You cannot live for God until you learn how to live because of God. And you can't go and make good choices for God until you understand the gospel that says the choices you make don't make you who you are; what Christ has done for you makes you who you are.*
>
> —MICHAEL M. DONEHEY, address at Tenth Avenue North concert, 2010

It's easy to make jokes about it, but when I look back at those days, weeks, and months of pain and betrayal and struggle to just get through the day, I see a peaceful woman. I see a woman who was so much closer to the Lord than she ever thought possible; a woman who loved the Lord, who craved Scripture, who walked with a measure of grace that could have only come from the Holy Spirit.

But when things went from bad to worse, I became fearful. I was afraid of failing at this new path God had called me to walk. And yet I knew that God wouldn't give me more than His grace would enable me to bear. His purpose wasn't to destroy me but to give me just enough "too much" so that I turned to Him. I could only do this life by depending fully on Him.

Jesus isn't a break-glass-when-needed kind of Savior. Jesus is a need-You-every-millisecond Savior. And a don't-try-this-alone Savior. By relying on Him, we can do this life. We might be messes, but our lives will be well-lived messes that glorify God.

BECOMING MORE LIKE CHRIST

In the midst of abandonment and divorce, I think it's important for us to share openly about how difficult this path is for us. It's challenging, and it's easy to become overwhelmed and look away from God as if there is a better option out there. Please, learn from my mistakes. There is no better option than God. Actually, there is no option other than God. He is it. I cannot imagine living this life without the Lord's peace and hope.

Let God use this experience in your life to make you more like Christ. Let Him pour His Spirit into you with abandon. Let Him lavish you with His love. It truly is the best love out there, no matter what the world tells you about romance. The world's view of romantic love is a counterfeit. Know His real love. Know Him. Fall in love with Jesus. He will pour refreshment into your soul. He will heal your broken heart and bind up your wounds (Psalm 147:3). He is "near to the brokenhearted and saves the crushed in spirit" (Psalm 34:18, ESV).

Jesus is more than able to take your burdens, more than willing to carry you, more than hopeful that you will allow Him to be your Savior. Allow Him into your life—into all the things you are trying to handle on your own, all the things you can't figure out, all the overwhelming moments of your day, and all the relationships with people who need you. Remember when I said that as single parents, we need to accept help from those around us? Well, inviting the Lord into your life is so much more important than anything another person can do for you, no matter how helpful.

That dinner prepared for us by a friend is a blessing, but the true, lifelong blessing lies in a heart that hopes in the Lord's steadfast love and trusts that God only allows in our lives those things that will make us better, stronger, and more able to bless those around us. I want to be that kind of woman. I want my children to rise up and call me blessed

(Proverbs 31:28, ESV). I want my friends and neighbors to be inspired by my life—inspired to know Christ. I want people to see Jesus instead of me. I want people to not even think about me as much as they think about Him, because they know that He is my identity (Galatians 2:20).

> But you, O LORD, are
> a shield about me, my
> glory, and the lifter of my
> head. I cried aloud to the
> LORD, and he answered
> me from his holy hill. I
> lay down and slept;
> I woke again, for the
> LORD sustained me.
>
> —PSALM 3:3–5, ESV

This new me might occasionally be a stumbling, fumbling mess of a sinner, but I'm on the road to knowing my Savior better. I'm determined that I will run this race set before me with grace, faith, and strength from the Lord (1 Corinthians 9:24). I might feel weak and inadequate, and I might be fearful and anxious, but "God is the strength of my heart and my portion forever" (Psalm 73:26). I believe I can do all that God has called me to do. And I believe you can, too.

LOOKING AHEAD TO A LIFE LIVED FEARLESSLY

So who am I going to become in the midst of this life? What kind of woman, mother, friend, daughter? How am I going to survive when most of the time I'm working off the fumes of the fumes? I'll tell you! I'm going to speak some truths into my life—get them firmly into my head and heart. I encourage you to do the same. I'm going to be a woman who walks with my head held high because I know that God's love is unfailing (Psalm 33:18–22). I'm going to be a woman who isn't afraid of the future, because I trust that God has it all handled, and it's going to be good. I'm not going to be a woman who is anxious about my children, because I know that God loves them just as He loves me (1 Peter 5:7). I'm going to be a woman who doesn't fear loneliness, because I have my constant companion and friend Jesus (Hebrews 13:5).

I made the following list while going through my divorce. I've lost sight of it more times than I care to admit. I'm showing it to you so that you can make your own. Who do you want to be at the end of this journey?

I want to be . . .

A woman of faith

A woman of the Word

A quiet and gentle-spirited woman (1 Peter 3:4)

A woman who holds her tongue (Proverbs 10:19)

A woman who listens (James 1:19)

A woman who overflows with the fruit of the Spirit: love, joy, peace, patience, kindness, goodness, faithfulness, gentleness, and self control (Galatians 5:22–23)

A woman whose children know they are loved and feel nurtured

A woman whose children are devoted to God

A woman whose home is organized, inviting, and loving

A woman whose finances are in order

A woman whose life is a reflection of God's faithfulness

A woman who is good to her friends

A generous woman

A kind-hearted woman

A worshipful woman

A loving woman

A woman who bears with others

A woman who is physically fit

A woman who is healthy—emotionally, physically, and spiritually

A woman who knows her Savior loves her

A woman who is secure in her walk with the Lord

A woman whose children know the Lord and study His Word

A woman who seeks the Lord

A woman who shares her gifts, wisdom, and possessions

A woman who is forgiving and loved

Each day I'm blessed to sense God leading me still. As a single parent, I rely on the Lord to show me how to best raise my children with strength and joy. Because I have a relationship with the Lord, I never truly feel alone. Sometimes I still struggle even after I pray, study, and seek counsel. Sometimes the answers and comfort don't come instantly; that's when I must exercise my faith—trusting what I don't see, believing what I don't always feel, and hoping for better things.

I might have moments of feeling overwhelmed, but I need only to bow my head and seek God's peace to find comfort. I might have no idea how to handle a particular situation or make a certain decision, but I know that when I seek His help through prayer, Bible study, and godly counsel, I will find a way to do the best thing. I might feel sorrow and deep pain over all that has happened, but God has comforted me through His Word and the kindness of friends and family. He hasn't left me alone to fend for myself in this trauma. He won't forsake me, and He won't forsake you.

I'm praying for you, my friend. How thankful I am that God has allowed us to walk this path together. I know that our stories are not exactly the same, but as we share our struggles and heartbreak, God can work mightily to bring healing and encouragement. I pray that this book has done that for you.

I know that recovering from hurts such as adultery, abandonment, or divorce is an upward battle, but it is God's battle. Be encouraged that God is trustworthy, and He will never be thwarted in fulfilling His good and perfect plan for your life or mine. I know He is going to do wondrous things in our lives as we trust in Him!

Father, our Lord and Savior, we come before You longing to know Your love to our core, Your mercy in our hearts, Your grace in every situation, Your Word in our heads. Oh, God, please bless us with Your peace, which surpasses understanding and guards our hearts and minds in Christ Jesus (Philippians 4:6–7). Father, reveal Yourself as our perfect Spouse and our children's perfect Parent. Lord, hold us close and sustain us. Bless us with strength for the day and hope for the future. Thank You for all that You are going to do in our lives, the many ways You are going to show Your faithfulness and care (Psalm 68:5). Thank You that You have a great plan for our lives and the lives of our children. May our children always keep their focus on You! May we always keep our focus on You!

In Jesus' name, amen.

ACKNOWLEDGMENTS

Each day I'm more and more aware of how loved I am by my Lord! Each day I'm in awe of His faithfulness and grace toward me and mine. I will forever be grateful to Him. "The LORD is my strength and my shield; my heart trusts in him, and I am helped. My heart leaps for joy and I will give thanks to him in song" (Psalm 28:7).

Thank you to my family for all your love and care—Mom and Dad (El and Alice Birdseye), James and Debbie Birdseye, Donald and Miho Birdseye, Sarah and Andrew Vaas, and Elizabeth Castro.

I cannot begin to express the depth of my love and gratitude to my dearest friends who have never left my side and have walked by me and my children with strength, encouragement, grace, and love from day one to today—David and Maria Copeland, John and Joanna Winters, Jonas and Darcey Geissler, Daniel and Sharon Donehey, Steve and Muriel May, Pamela Lopes, and Robert and Carol Becker.

To my sweet friends who loved me in more ways than I could have imagined possible and who have prayed for me diligently—Tim and Cheryl Curtis, Matt and Jennifer May, Kirk and Angela Dunmire, James and Cindy Richters, Todd and Candy Rowley, Mike and Kathleen Lewis, Matt and Daphne Phillips, James and Elizabeth Sparks, Mark and Phoebe Rist, Matt and Kati Malloy, Bill and Laurie Britt, Jeff and Amy Cox, Allison Jerden, Bethanie Cooke, Mike and Carol Taylor, John and Lynda Mersiovsky, Deanna Sawyer, Donna Hitt, Lee Bjornsen, Elaine Ramos, John Piser, Julie Weems, Kathryn Pugh, Kirk and Stephanie Ross, Lisa Tate, Meg Ulfers, David and Melody Leeper, Robert McWethy, Gregory O'Toole, Doc Murdock, Molly Donehey, Nancy Coleman, Sandee Cogan,

Sara Dunn, Sara Sexton, Stacie Bard, Robert Azzarito, Daniel Comber, Josh and Alice Howell, and my New City Fellowship Church family.

I know there are so many more—so many people who have touched our lives. Please know that nothing went unnoticed, and I thank my God for all of you.

Thank you to my kind and encouraging editor, Brandy Bruce. I appreciate all the time you invested in this book and all the ways you challenged me, strengthened me, and were patient with me. You are a blessing to be sure!

Thank you to the publishing team at Focus on the Family and to Tyndale House Publishers for being willing to take on this book. What a tremendous honor to work with you!

And to my friend Shaunti Feldhahn, who has known me since I was a little girl and loved me even still. Thank you for inspiring me to take this journey and experience the blessing of watching God make it into something for His glory and my good!